Future Scenarios

A Technical Document Supporting
the Forest Service 2010 RPA Assessment

Abstract: The Forest and Rangeland Renewable Resources Planning Act of 1974 (RPA) mandates a periodic assessment of the conditions and trends of the Nation's renewable resources on forests and rangelands. The RPA Assessment includes projections of resource conditions and trends 50 years into the future. The 2010 RPA Assessment used a set of future scenarios to provide a unifying framework for resources analyses. Those scenarios, and their associated assumptions about population change, economic growth, land use change, bioenergy, and climate change, are described in this document.

Keywords: scenarios, population, income, land use, bioenergy, climate

Acknowledgments

We would like to acknowledge the primary authors of this report: Amy E. Daniels, Linda A. Joyce, and Linda L. Langner. We also acknowledge that sections of the report are drawn from more detailed RPA Assessment supporting documents authored by H. Ken Cordell, Peter J. Ince, Linda A. Joyce, David N. Wear, and Stanley J. Zarnoch.

We thank our peer reviewers for their excellent suggestions: David Darr (retired Forest Service), William Goran (U.S. Army Corps of Engineers), James Hrubovcak (USDA Office of Chief Economist), Jeffrey Kline (U.S. Forest Service Pacific Northwest Research Station), and Jan Lewandrowski (USDA Climate Change Program Office). Reviews by Ross Arnold, Margaret Connelly, Curtis Flather, and Guy Robertson also greatly improved the document.

We also acknowledge the World Climate Research Program for their role in contributing and willingness to share the Coupled Model Intercomparison Project phase 3 (CMIP3) multi-model dataset through the Program for Climate Model Diagnosis and Intercomparison web portal. We also wish to acknowledge the efforts of the IPCC Data Distribution Centre (DDC) to archive and share the IPCC Third Assessment climate projection data. And we acknowledge the following modeling groups for the availability of their data: the Canadian Centre for Climate Modeling and Analysis, the Commonwealth Scientific and Industrial Research Organisation in Australia, the Hadley Centre for Climate Prediction and Research in the UK, and in Japan, the Centre for Climate System Research (CCSR), together with the University of Tokyo, and the National Institute for Environmental Studies and the Frontier Research Center for Global Change.

Contents

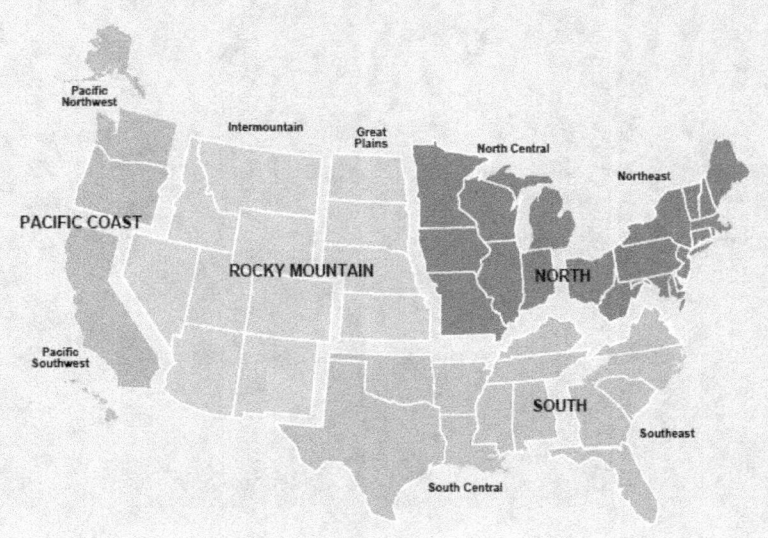

Introduction

The Forest and Rangeland Renewable Resources Planning Act of 1974 (RPA) (P.L. 93-378, 88 Stat 475, as amended) mandates a periodic assessment of the condition and trends of the Nation's renewable resources on forests and rangelands. The RPA Assessment provides a snapshot of current United States (U.S.) forest and rangeland conditions and trends on all ownerships, identifies drivers of change, and projects 50 years into the future. We analyze trends in outdoor recreation, fish and wildlife, biological diversity, wilderness, forests, range, water, urban forests, landscape patterns, and the potential effects of climate change on these resources.

The 2010 RPA Assessment is the fifth assessment prepared in response to this mandate (U.S. Forest Service 1977, 1981, 1989, 2001). This report describes the framework for the 2010 RPA Assessment, describes the future scenarios, and documents the common assumptions used across resource analyses.

Framework for the 2010 RPA Assessment

The framing of the RPA Assessment has evolved to respond to changes in natural resource issues and management. The original legislation focused primarily on an economic evaluation of whether resource supplies could meet consumer demands. As public expectations about the role of natural resources broadened to include both ecological and socioeconomic considerations, the RPA Assessment analyses also broadened to assess resource conditions, ecosystem health, and sustainability in recognition of the interrelationships between ecological and socioeconomic conditions in meeting the expectations of the American public. While maintaining the ability to report on economic supply and demand, this broader and more flexible approach improves our ability to evaluate the future of the Nation's forests and rangelands and adapt to changing information needs.[1]

---

[1] A description of previous RPA Assessments and the supporting publications can be found at http://www fs fed.us/research/rpa/what. shtml.

The 2010 RPA Assessment framework was designed to:

- incorporate global interactions that affect domestic resource conditions and trends,
- improve analyses of interactions among resources,
- extend our analytical capability to evaluate the potential effects of climate change across the resources, and
- describe more clearly the complexity and uncertainty associated with projecting future conditions and trends.

Global Linkages

Global conditions and trends increasingly affect the conditions and trends in domestic natural resources. The international context has always been considered in RPA Assessment analyses, mainly in terms of the supply and demand of wood products. The international context is important in other areas, such as destination travel for recreation, energy policies, and wildlife. The 2010 framework improved these linkages through two main changes. First, the 2010 RPA Assessment used a set of future scenarios for the United States tied to a global set of scenarios that provide a coherent interdependent future for global and U.S. population dynamics, socioeconomic factors and climate change for more than 50 years into the future. These scenarios provided both quantitative and qualitative connections for the domestic resource analyses that project resource conditions and trends for 50 years. Second, the U.S. forest resource assessment nested the U.S. domestic forest products model within a global forest trade model quantitatively tied to the global IPCC scenarios.

Resource Interactions

Many common stressors impact renewable resources and create interactive effects between them. The 2010 analyses continued the practice of using common historical and projected data for U.S. population, economic growth, and land use change across individual resource analyses. These socioeconomic variables continue to be important drivers of resource change. The 2010 RPA Assessment added a common historical and projected data set for climate variables, which ensured consistency in incorporating climate effects in resource models,

USDA Forest Service Gen. Tech. Rep. RMRS-GTR-272. 2012

1

including models for forest inventory projections, water yield/use projections, and recreation use projections.

The individual resource analyses for the RPA Assessment are primarily done with a series of independent models. The main exception is the forest resource modeling system, which has linkages between land use, forest inventory, and forest products. The common assumptions about population growth, economic growth, land use change, bioenergy use, and climate change are used to ensure that all resource projections are based on the same drivers of change. The use of the common assumptions provides opportunities to create feedback loops across the resource analyses.

Potential Effects of Climate Change

A 1990 amendment to the RPA legislation—the only substantive amendment to the Assessment mandate since enactment—required the Assessment to analyze potential effects of global climate change on renewable resources and to identify mitigation opportunities. The first RPA "climate" report was a special report summarizing current knowledge of the effects of climate change on forests (Joyce and others 1990). The 1993 RPA Assessment update included the first analysis linking climate projections with an ecological model to drive productivity changes in a timber assessment model at a national scale (Joyce 1995). This timber policy model also linked to a carbon accounting model to track carbon inventory of U.S. forests. The 2000 RPA Assessment made further advances, including ecological models that expanded our capacity to look not only at productivity shifts but also ecosystem type shifts (Joyce and Birdsey 2000). Other advances included refined estimates of all carbon pools associated with the U.S. forests and wood products for the U.S. carbon inventory and a more detailed analysis of the implications of forest management on carbon sequestration.

The 2010 RPA Assessment took a fundamentally different approach to examine the effects of climate change. A consistent set of U.S. future scenarios were developed which include projections for population, economic activity, climate, and bioenergy. Where possible, the resource models were revamped to directly include climate variables in the same manner that socioeconomic and biological variables are used to project future resource effects. The climate projections were driven by the scenarios described in the scenarios approach section.

Complexity and Uncertainty

The RPA Assessment analyses address a wide range of economic and ecological phenomena. Individually, the economic, social, and biological systems that affect the provisioning of goods and services are quite complex. Integrating effects across these systems adds additional complexity. Considerable uncertainty is also associated with projections of the future, particularly projections that look forward 50 years. Past RPA Assessments typically focused on one "business as usual" future, with varying assumptions about future population sometimes being used to create high/medium/low trajectories of supply and demand. In addition, the timber assessment often included various alternative futures linked to different policy and/or trade assumptions. Common assumptions were used for population change, economic growth rates, and land use change. Climate change analyses were restricted to effects on timber markets and forest resources.

Using global scenarios to frame the 2010 analyses provided a coherent framework for evaluating outcomes across resource analyses. Socioeconomic and climate variables were all linked through these global scenarios. Scenarios were not assigned likelihoods, nor were any scenarios intended to be "accurate" *per se*. Rather, these constructed scenarios provided a means of qualitatively and quantitatively understanding (a) how different socioeconomic processes interacted to create different possible greenhouse gas (GHG) emissions pathways, (b) how these emissions pathways drove global climate models to project different potential future climates, and (c) how various natural resources would respond to alternative future climates. Each link in this chain of models is subject to uncertainty from a number of sources ranging from deliberate modeling assumptions (for example, the global population growth rate selected for a given scenario), to stochastic processes in the global climate, economic, and biological systems themselves. The purpose of using future scenarios to drive different resource projections for the 2010 RPA Assessment was to facilitate exploring a consistent range of possible futures across resource analyses rather than intending to actually predict future resource conditions.

Figure 1 presents a schematic that illustrates how global scenarios were linked to U.S. data used in the various RPA resource analyses. The remainder of this document will focus on the topics in the box labeled "Basic

2

USDA Forest Service Gen. Tech. Rep. RMRS-GTR-272. 2012

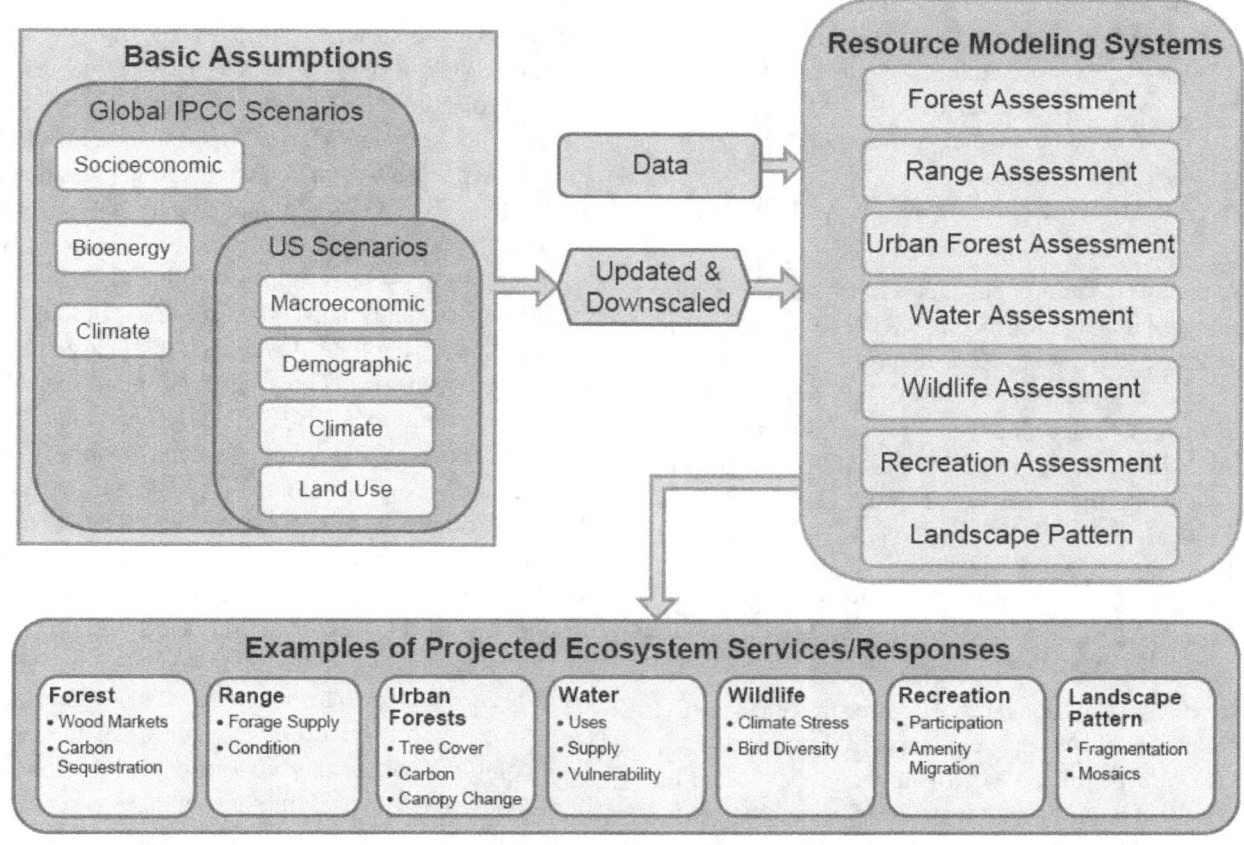

Figure 1—RPA Assessment scenario analysis and modeling systems.

Assumptions." The next section provides details on the selection of scenarios for the 2010 RPA analyses, followed by descriptions of the components of the assumptions including population, economics, bioenergy, land use, and climate. The underlying assumptions described in this document are key inputs to the resource analyses listed in the "Resource Modeling Systems" box. The outcome of these analyses is the estimation of future goods and services from forests and rangelands, with examples shown in the bottom box of figure 1.

Scenario Approach in the 2010 RPA Assessment

Scenarios are used to explore alternative futures and are intended to serve as a counterfactual framework for objectively evaluating a plausible range of future resource outcomes. This approach is particularly useful when there is considerable uncertainty about the trajectory of the driving forces behind political, economic, social, and ecological changes (Alcamo and others 2003, IPCC 2007). A scenario approach can use both qualitative and quantitative approaches in visualizing alternative futures using different socioeconomic or institutional assumptions for the United States. Carpenter and others (2005) and Nakicenovic and others (2000) review examples and uses of scenario analysis in other applications.

The challenge of incorporating global interactions in the 2010 RPA Assessment led to the search for a set of comprehensive global scenarios to serve as anchors for the RPA Assessment analyses. These global scenarios would provide the context and quantitative linkages between U.S. and global trends. We identified several criteria for evaluating and selecting global scenarios:

- Scenarios must be globally consistent.
- Scenarios must be scientifically credible and well-documented.

USDA Forest Service Gen. Tech. Rep. RMRS-GTR-272. 2012

3

- Scenarios must include assumptions about key driving forces of resource change:
    - o Population and economic growth
    - o Land use change
    - o Climate change
    - o Energy use
- Globally consistent data must be available to link to U.S.-scale analyses.

We reviewed a number of scenario-based approaches as potential anchors for the 2010 RPA Assessment: the Millennium Ecosystem Assessment (Alcamo and others 2003, Carpenter and others 2005), the Intergovernmental Panel on Climate Change (IPCC) (Nakicenovic and others 2000), the "Mapping the Global Future" project (National Intelligence Council 2004), and the United Nations Environmental Program's Global Environmental Outlook (UNEP 2002, 2007). Although these studies exhibited wide variations in approach and objectives, all focused on a similar set of driving forces that shape the global future.

We selected emissions scenarios used in both the IPCC third and fourth Assessment Reports (known as TAR and AR4, respectively) to provide the global scenarios for the 2010 RPA Assessment. The Special Report on Emissions Scenarios (SRES) from the TAR (Nakicenovic and others 2000) provides detailed documentation of these scenarios. The overwhelming advantage of using these IPCC emissions scenarios as the basis for the 2010 RPA Assessment was the level of scientific rigor and acceptance surrounding their development, the degree of documentation, and the facilitated access to the data. The availability of socioeconomic and associated climate data at global, regional, and country scales was a critical decision factor. The range of scenarios considered in the IPCC Assessments provided a broad spectrum of potential futures from which we could select a subset to evaluate potential U.S. future resource conditions and trends.

IPCC Storylines and Emissions Scenarios

Established in 1988 as a scientific intergovernmental body, the IPCC assesses the latest scientific, technical, and socioeconomic literature relevant to understanding the risk of human-induced climate change, its observed and projected impacts, and options for adaptation and mitigation (http://www.ipcc.ch/about/index.htm). The IPCC produced its first Assessment Report in 1990; its second Assessment Report in 1995; the TAR in 2001; and the AR4 in 2007. These IPCC assessments revolve around projections, and associated implications, of how different socioeconomic scenarios translate into GHG emissions pathways that feed into global circulation models (GCMs). GCMs simulate climate change resulting from the varying concentrations of GHG as specified by different emissions scenarios. While the emphasis of the IPCC is climate change, the usefulness of the IPCC assessments for the RPA Assessment was based on the linkage between socioeconomic and climate variables.

Several generations of IPCC-developed emissions scenarios exist, each increasing in sophistication. Emissions scenarios developed for the TAR and AR4 represent the latest. Similarly, each successive IPCC assessment represents advancements in the GCMs developed by the nearly two-dozen major climate modeling groups around the world. To obtain the kinds of projected climate variables useful as inputs to RPA analyses, a specific emissions scenario must be selected and paired as a "driver" of a specific GCM, resulting in many possible combinations. In the sections below, we describe the TAR/AR4 IPCC storylines and emissions scenarios and our process for selecting emissions scenarios for the 2010 RPA Assessment.

IPCC storylines

The IPCC based the TAR and AR4 on a set of four storylines depicting potential future states of the world. The storylines are qualitative descriptions of the world that are internally consistent stories about how the future might evolve. The four families of storylines developed for use in the TAR and AR4 were A1, A2, B1, and B2. Within the A1 storyline, sub-storylines focused on different future uses of energy sources: A1B (balanced energy), A1F1 (fossil fuel intensive), and A1T (predominantly non-fossil fuel).

The storylines can be grossly characterized and categorized by assumptions about global population and gross domestic product (GDP) (table 1). Nakicenovic and others (2000) provide the full documentation of the storylines.

The A1 storyline describes a 21st century of very rapid economic growth with a global population that peaks in mid-century and then declines. The A1F1 scenario carries through a fossil-fuel intensive economy for as

4

USDA Forest Service Gen. Tech. Rep. RMRS-GTR-272. 2012

Table 1—Global population and Gross Domestic Product (GDP) projections for IPCC storylines, 2010-2100.

Storyline	2010	2020	2040	2060	2100
	Global population (millions)				
A1	6,805	7,493	8,439	8,538	7,056
A2	7,188	8,206	10,715	12,139	15,068
B1	6,892	7,618	8,547	8,671	7,047
B2	6,891	7,672	8,930	9,704	10,414
	Global GDP (2006 trillion USD)				
A1	54.2	80.6	181.8	336.2	756.5
A2	45.6	57.9	103.4	145.7	347.2
B1	53.3	75.2	144.0	245.5	469.6
B2	67.1	72.5	133.3	195.6	335.9

long as possible, while A1T makes the shift to non-fossil intensive technology more rapidly than A1F1 or A1B. The A1B option within this storyline takes a more balanced approach between dependence on fossil fuel and early switching to other energy sources, so that the A1F1 and A1T scenarios tend to bracket the results of A1B.

The A2 storyline has a continuously increasing global population and more regionally oriented economic growth. It has the highest global population growth, but the lowest long-term economic growth. The emissions are less than A1F1, but higher than A1T.

The B1 storyline shares the same population trend as A1, but with an economic future of rapid change toward a service and information economy and a strong emphasis on clean and resource-efficient technologies. GDP growth is lower, but the greatest divergence with A1 does not occur until after 2060.[2] Global GHG emissions are not very different between B1 and A1T.

The B2 storyline is similar to A2 in that regional and local institutions are emphasized over global integration, with intermediate economic growth and a growing global population. Per capita income is comparable to A2 and B1, but population growth is significantly lower than all other scenarios. B2 also has the lowest projected growth in biomass energy in the global region that includes the United States.

Emissions scenarios

The IPCC storylines were then used to develop emissions scenarios for the TAR and AR4. Quantifying the population and GDP projections of each storyline transformed the qualitative storylines into quantitative emissions scenarios evaluated through six integrated assessment models (IAMs). For each of the four storylines (A1, A2, B1, and B2) and A1 sub-storylines (A1B, A1F1, A1T), IAM modeling teams used the population and GDP projections specified by the storyline and then proceeded to further interpret, model, and quantify other necessary variables for estimating GHG emissions consistent with the storyline. For example, modeling teams developed quantitative assumptions about technology change, energy sources, and land use change. Each IAM had a different "focus" (see Appendix A for more information about the six IAMs). Quantification of the storylines through IAMs resulted in a suite of 40 emissions scenarios across the four storylines that provided a broad range of future outcomes in terms of GHG emissions through 2100. Each emissions scenario was considered an equally possible future and linked different levels of GHG emissions to global environmental outcomes, including climate.

Each IAM group had the responsibility to create a "marker" emissions scenario for a storyline or sub-storyline. These marker emissions scenarios were harmonized, meaning they used common assumptions about the main driving forces within the storylines. Marker scenarios were not intended to be mean or median scenarios across the range of scenarios. Rather, they illustrated their respective storylines and were subjected

---

[2] The RPA Assessment projection period ends in 2060, while the IPCC AR4 projections end in 2100.

USDA Forest Service Gen. Tech. Rep. RMRS-GTR-272. 2012

5

to more intensive review and tests of reproducibility than the other emissions scenarios (Nakicenovic and others 2000). As such, marker scenarios are most widely used for the study of climate change impacts and other applications.

To reiterate an important point, none of the storylines or emissions scenarios were considered to reflect the "most likely" or "business as usual" future. The TAR and AR4 deliberately avoided judging the likelihood of future scenarios. Although covering a wide range of alternative futures, the storylines and resulting emissions scenarios deliberately excluded global disaster scenarios. Scenarios simply provide a tool to explore a range of future outcomes without judgment about the desirability of the outcomes (Nakicenovic and others 2000).

Selecting the Scenarios and Climate Models for the 2010 RPA Assessment

Selecting the scenarios

We analyzed the variation across the marker scenarios, evaluating the range of variation in world population, U.S. population, world and U.S. GDP, energy futures, and climate. We had no pre-determined test of what constitutes "sufficient" variation in any of the variables, so the basic test was whether a subset of the IPCC scenarios would cover the range of possibilities that were likely to drive the greatest variation in resource effects in the United States. The B1 storyline was dropped from consideration because its population trajectory matched A1, and the differences in GDP growth did not diverge greatly until after 2060. We initially proposed using the following four IPCC storylines/scenarios: A1FI, A1T, A2, and B2. However, no marker scenario was developed for either A1FI or A1T; the marker scenario was developed for A1B in the A1 family.

After our initial selection of scenarios, we checked on the availability of climate projections linked to the marker scenarios. In planning for the AR4, the climate model community, through the World Climate Research Programme's Working Group on Coupled Modelling, organized a coordinated set of experiments exploring climate variability and change that could be performed by modeling groups with state-of-the art global coupled climate models. These coordinated and structured experiments conducted by a diversity of modeling groups

facilitated a greater understanding of climate and climate modeling. A critical part of this process was the archiving of climate model output data so that the international climate science community would have access for analysis (Meehl and others 2007a), which was undertaken by the Program for Climate Model Diagnosis and Intercomparison (PCMDI). Choices about the experiments influenced the availability of the scenario-based climate projections. The list of experiments included only the emissions scenarios A1B, A2, and B1 (Meehl and others 2007a). Consequently, no climate projections for A1T, A1FI, or B2 scenarios were archived through PCMDI (http://www-pcmdi.llnl.gov/ipcc/data_status_tables.htm). As a result we decided to use the A1B scenario instead of A1T and A1FI. We did not want to drop the B2 scenario, so we turned to the TAR archived projections for B2.

Selecting the climate models

Scenario A2 shows the greatest global warming of 3.4 degrees C by 2100, followed by A1B with 2.8 degrees C and B2 with 2.4 degrees C when averaged across all AR4 models (IPCC 2007). Not only do projections of the global surface warming vary by emissions scenario over the next 100 years, the projections vary by the individual climate model. Based on an analysis of a variety of different climate models, the uncertainty for each of these scenarios can range from nearly 1 degree C below the average to 2 degrees C above the average; for example, for the 3.4 degree C mean of the A2 scenario, the uncertainty range is 2.0 to 5.4 degrees C (Meehl and others 2007b). Individual climate models reflect a common understanding of climate processes held by the international community and also individual understanding of these processes by each modeling group. Hence the models respond slightly differently when forced by the atmospheric chemistry projected for the future. Since the results varied by GCM within each scenario, we considered it important to identify several climate models to include in the RPA analyses to provide variation in the resource projections based on climate variables.

We selected AR4 climate models that developed global projections for A1B and A2 from the PCMDI Climate Model Intercomparison Project 3 (CMIP3) website, and the TAR climate models that developed global projections for B2 from the IPCC Date Distribution Centre. Three GCMs were chosen for each marker scenario based on

6

USDA Forest Service Gen. Tech. Rep. RMRS-GTR-272. 2012

the availability of the projections in the CMIP3 database at the time this study started and the variables needed for the RPA Assessment and assessments being done in Canada (Price and others 2011) (table 2). For the TAR climate models, a suite of climate models projecting the B2 scenario had been downscaled using the same procedure described here and had been used to assess the impact of climate effects on vegetation (Bachelet and others 2008, Price and others 2004). Hence these same models were selected. The global projections from these models capture a range of future climates.

The reliability of individual climate models has been explored using several different approaches: how well they simulate historical climate, whether they capture well-known regional climate phenomena such as the El Nino-Southern Oscillation, or how sensitive they are to the GHG changes. The three AR4 models used in this current study were included in the Multi-Model Data study that tested the climate sensitivity across GCMs (Randall and others 2007): CGCM3.1, MIROC3.2, and UKMO_HADCM3. Their climate sensitivities were about and above the mean. Reichler and Kim (2008) attempted to quantify agreement between model and observations for several generations of climate models. They conclude that the ability to simulate present-day mean climate has improved over these three generations. The most recent generation represented in AR4 would generally simulate present day climate more realistically than the models associated with TAR. In their approach, index values less than one indicate more accurate models, and the three AR4 models used in this study fall at or below one in their study.

Table 2—IPCC scenarios and GCM climate models used for the 2010 RPA Assessment.

Scenario	Integrated Assessment Model (IAM)	GCMs[1]	Model Vintage
A1B	AIM	CGCM3.1(T47) MIROC3.2(medres) CSIRO-Mk3.5	AR4
A2	ASF	CGCM3.1(T47) MIROC3.2(medres) CSIRO-Mk3.5	AR4
B2	MESSAGE	CGCM2 CSIRO-Mk2 UKMO-HadCM3	TAR

[1] CGCM3.1—Canadian Centre for Climate Modeling and Analysis (CCCma) Coupled Global Climate Model (CGCM3), Medium Resolution (T47). http://www.cccma. bc.ec.gc.ca/models/cgcm3.shtml

CSIRO-Mk3.5—Commonwealth Scientific and Industrial Research Organization (CSIRO) (Australia), CSIRO Mk3 Climate System Model. http://www.cmar.csiro.au/e-print/ open/gordon_2002a.pdf

MIROC3.2MR—Center for Climate System Research (CCSR), University of Tokyo; National Institute for Environmental Studies (NIES) and Frontier Research Center for Global Change (FRCGC) (Japan), Model for Interdisciplinary Research on Climate (MIROC) Version 3.2 Medium Resolution. http://www.ccsr.u-tokyo.ac.jp/ kyosei/hasumi/MIROC/tech-repo.pdf

CGCM2—Coupled Global Climate Model, Medium Resolution (T47). Canadian Centre for Climate Modelling and Analysis http://www.cccma.bc.ec.gc.ca/models/cgcm2.shtml

CSIRO-Mk2—Australia's Commonwealth Scientific and Industrial Research Organisation Australia (CSIRO) http://www.cmar.csiro.au/e-print/open/hennessy_1998a. html#ccm

UKMO-HadCM3—Hadley Centre for Climate Prediction and Research UK (HCCPR) http:// cera-www.dkrz.de/IPCC_DDC/IS92a/HadleyCM3/hadcm3.html

USDA Forest Service Gen. Tech. Rep. RMRS-GTR-272. 2012

7

Scaling and Updating IPCC Data to U.S. and Sub-National Scales

The combination of an emissions scenario and a GCM provided the global demographic, macroeconomic, and climate assumptions for the various component analyses comprising the 2010 RPA Assessment. Here we describe the procedures used to develop national and sub-national projections of population, GDP, income, bioenergy use, land use change, and climate for the U.S. and RPA regions (figure 2) that are linked to the IPCC Assessment.

The IPCC scenario-based projections provided data at the global and macro-region level (Appendix B), with further disaggregation to the country level for population and GDP. The socioeconomic data from the IPCC marker scenarios served as drivers of the selected GCMs, which were then downscaled for RPA Assessment climate projections. We chose to update the IPCC projections of U.S. population and GDP projections with more recent U.S. data. In doing so, we maintained the trends and cross-scenario relationships of IPCC scenarios as explained below. We disaggregated these updated estimates to obtain county-level income and population data for the RPA Assessment analyses.

Projecting population and economic information at the county-level involved a number of simplifying assumptions. Accounting for the various state and local events that govern the change and development of towns and counties is impossible. As a result, the RPA county-level projections presented here for the national assessment should not be taken as statistically reliable projections of possible economic or demographic futures for specific counties. Rather, the overall spatial pattern of change in response to alternative scenarios is more important in our analyses, displaying the heterogeneity that would not be evident if projections were made only at RPA regional or national levels.

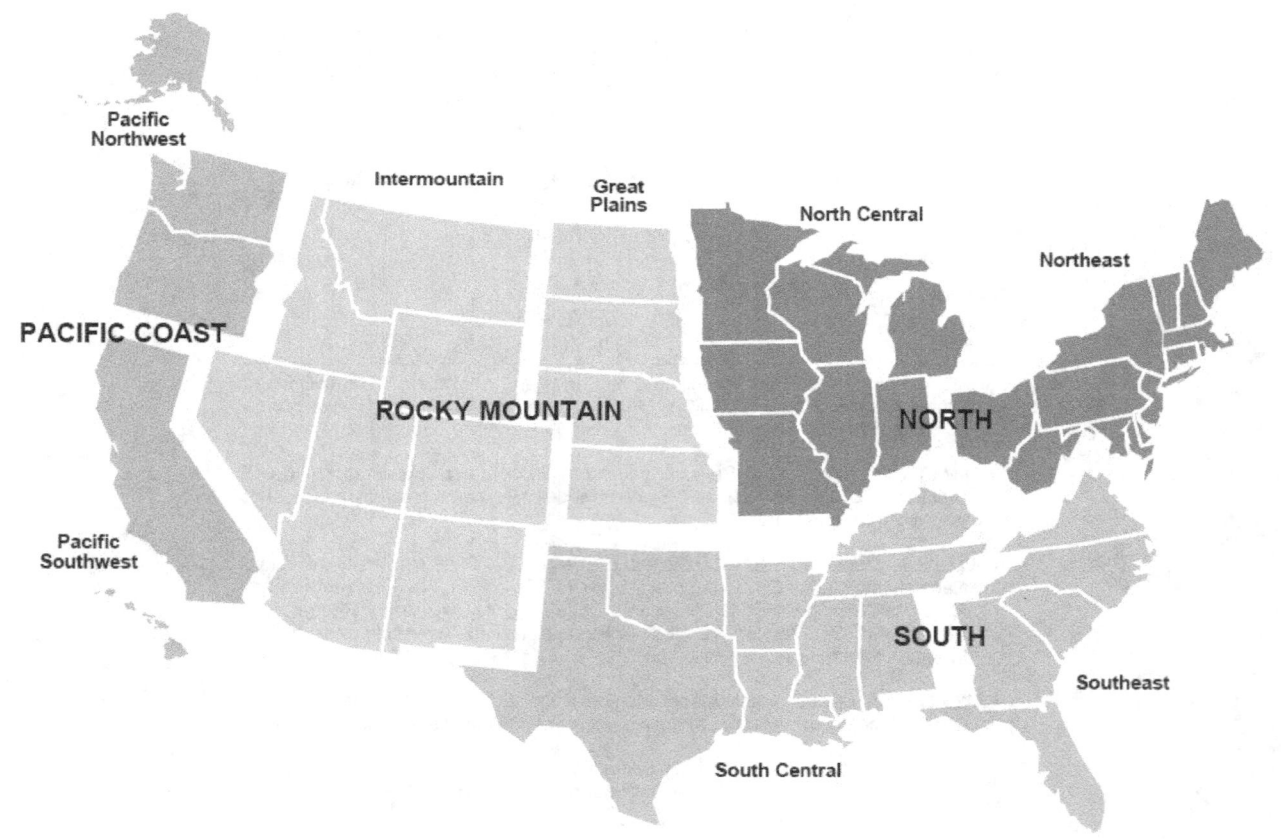

Figure 2—RPA Assessment regions.

8

USDA Forest Service Gen. Tech. Rep. RMRS-GTR-272. 2012

U.S. Population Projections

The IPCC A1B population projections for the United States were based on 1990 Census Bureau projections. The 1990 Census projections are lower than more recent Census projections (U.S. Census Bureau 2004). Therefore, we used the 2004 Census population series for 2000-2050 to replace the original IPCC U.S. population projection for A1B. The difference in U.S. population is quite small from an IPCC regional or global perspective, but population is a strong driver of resource change for the United States. Therefore, updating the U.S. data for A1B to match the newer Census projections was important. Since Census projections ended in 2050, we extrapolated the Census projection to 2060, the end of the RPA projection period.

The 2004 Census population projection (with the extrapolation to 2060) served as the U.S. population projection for the RPA A1B scenario. We then revised the population projections for the A2 and B2 storylines to begin at the same starting point as the updated A1B. The A2 and B2 projections were adjusted relative to the updated A1B projection to maintain the same proportional relationship as among the original IPCC projections. Table 3 shows the original IPCC U.S. population projections and the updated U.S. population projections for the 2010 RPA Assessment. Figure 3 illustrates the updated projections for the three RPA scenarios relative to historical population trends in the United States.

Table 3—IPCC U.S. population projections and updated RPA U.S. population projections, 2000- 2060 by scenario (millions of people).

	2000	2010	2020	2030	2040	2050	2060
IPCC							
A1B	277	300	324	347	367	383	396
A2	278	306	334	363	390	417	447
B2	278	299	322	337	343	348	351
RPA							
A1B	282	309	336	364	392	420	447
A2	282	315	346	380	416	457	505
B2	282	308	334	353	366	381	397

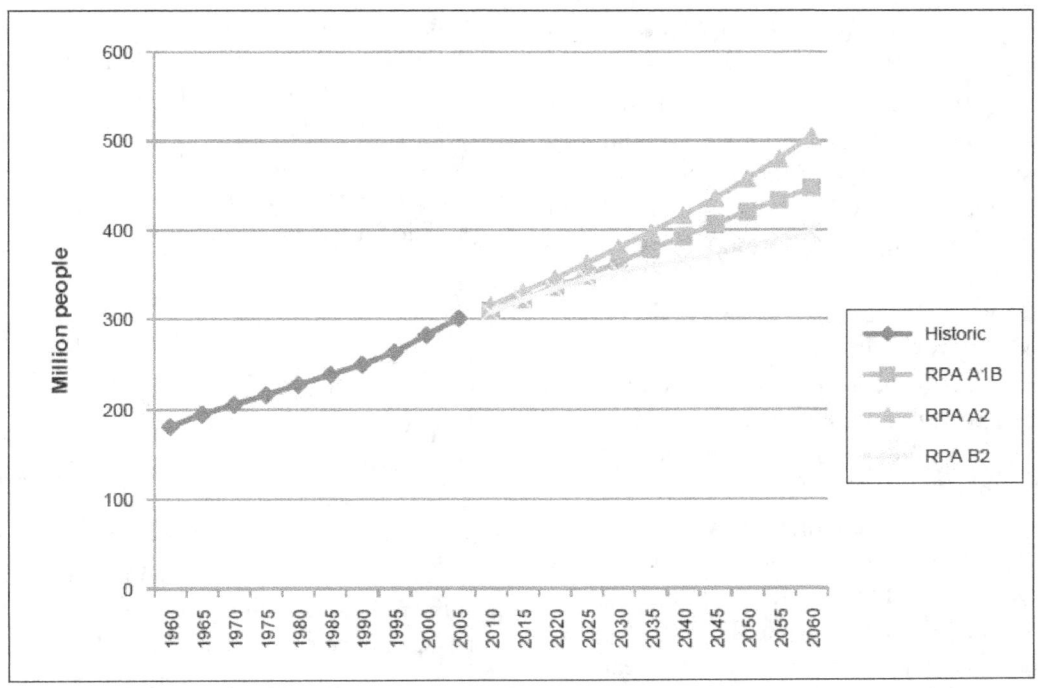

Figure 3—Historic U.S. population and projected U.S. population to 2060 by RPA scenario.

USDA Forest Service Gen. Tech. Rep. RMRS-GTR-272. 2012

9

U.S. population at the county level

A number of RPA Assessment analyses require county-level population projections. No readily available county-level projections exist that extend to 2060. Several commercial vendors offer county-level projections for a shorter time period, but these single projection series do not link to the scenarios chosen for the 2010 RPA Assessment. However, these types of projections can be a starting point for the RPA county-level projections. We describe the process for disaggregating the U.S. population projections to the county scale briefly below; detailed documentation is available in Zarnoch and others (2010).

We used the Woods & Poole Economics, Inc. (WP) projection series to provide the starting point for the county-level projections from 2010-2030 (Woods & Poole Economics Inc. 2006). From the WP county-level projections, we calculated county shares of the WP national population total, which differs slightly from the Census U.S. population total. Because Census projections were the basis for the adjusted A1B projection, we then applied the WP county shares to the Census U.S. population totals. The result was county-level population projections through 2030 based on the WP county shares, but that sum to the 2004 Census U.S. population projections.

The second step was to develop county-level projections from 2035-2060 in five-year time steps consistent with an extrapolation of the WP projection series and constrained by national population totals from A1B. The projections from 2035 to 2060 used the previous five to 10-year absolute growth for a given county and adjusted it such that the sum of the projections across all counties equaled the A1B-projected national total for that projection year. We performed this additivity adjustment for each time interval since the growth in the previous five to 10-year period may not necessarily have equaled the growth in the next period.

The additivity adjustment factor was either positive or negative. For a positive additivity adjustment factor, all counties with increasing populations had their growth increased by this factor. Similarly, all counties with decreasing populations had their growth decreased. The additivity adjustment factor for any of the five-year time steps was obtained by equating the A1B national population in that year to the sum of the increasing and decreasing county populations in the same year. The result was that both increasing and decreasing counties were adjusted with the same proportional adjustment. This adjustment only applied to the change in county population between time periods and not to the total county population. This ensured that increasing counties remained increasing and decreasing counties remained decreasing after adjustment.

Our system for these projections was simplistic and did not take into account natural density-dependent mechanisms that affect human demographic dynamics. As such, high density counties with high rates of growth exhibited explosive population increases while high density counties with high rates of negative growth tended toward complete depopulation. We developed a modification to dampen the extreme increases and decreases.

We defined three fast increasing groups and three fast decreasing groups based on each county's percentile rank for the two criteria, population density and density growth rate. These groups were then assigned dampening factors that would adjust their growth slightly by decreasing positive growth and decreasing negative growth. Experimenting with the cut points for these groups led to a set of final criteria for dampening factors and resulting population projections through their application.

We obtained county population projections from 2035-2060 for the A2 and B2 scenarios directly from the county shares from the A1B county projections using the same additivity adjustment and dampening methodology outlined previously. Using this approach, we preserved the proportionate relationship between projected total national population for the A1B, A2, and B2 scenarios. This assured that the three projections for a single county did not unexpectedly cross, which could occasionally occur if not constrained in this way.

U.S. Economic Projections

Macroeconomic outlook

Macroeconomic trends (for example, trends in GDP, disposable personal income, and labor productivity) have a critical influence on the supply of and demand for renewable resources. The IPCC projections of GDP were based on data developed in the early 1990s. Similar to the rationale for updating the U.S. population projections, we decided to update the GDP projections to reflect more current trends. Therefore, the U.S. GDP projections were updated with more current data, relative to the

10

USDA Forest Service Gen. Tech. Rep. RMRS-GTR-272. 2012

data used in the emissions scenarios, and all monetary projections were converted to 2006 USD instead of the original 1990 USD used in the emissions scenarios.

The Forest Service commissioned a U.S. macroeconomic outlook report from the Economic Research Service (ERS) to project U.S. macroeconomic trends through 2060[3]. We used the official U.S. GDP value for 2006 as the new starting point for the A1B, A2, and B2 projections (U.S. Department of Commerce 2008a). We used GDP growth rates projected in the ERS report to develop an updated projection of GDP for the A1B scenario. The updated GDP for A1B was slightly higher than the IPCC projection. We revised the A2 and B2 GDP projections to maintain the same proportional relationship to the updated A1B GDP trajectory as the one defined by the original IPCC GDP projections. Table 4 shows the differences between the original IPCC projections for U.S. GDP compared to the updated GDP figures, as well as the national-level projections for U.S. personal income and U.S. disposable personal income used in the RPA scenarios. Figure 4 shows the differences among the three RPA scenario projections for updated GDP in comparison to historical U.S. GDP.

U.S. income projections

GDP is a useful aggregate variable used primarily in the forest products models as a demand driver, but modeling choices at finer scales for other resources required a more disaggregated measure of economic growth. Measures of personal income and disposable personal income were used as drivers in other resource analyses, such as land use change, water use, and recreation use. Similar to the process used for updating the GDP projections, the official U.S. 2006 statistics for personal income (PI) and disposable personal income (DPI) were used to start the updated RPA projections (U.S. Department of Commerce 2008b).

The ERS macroeconomic report projected national growth rates in disposable personal income (DPI) through 2060. These growth rates were applied to both the 2006 PI and DPI starting point to derive projections for total national PI and DPI for the A1B scenario (table 4). We calculated the A2 and B2 projections for PI and DPI to maintain the same proportional relationship across scenarios that were used in calculating the trajectories for GDP.

---

[3] Torgerson, D. 2007. US macroeconomic projections to 2060. On file with the U.S. Forest Service Quantitative Sciences Staff.

Table 4—IPCC U.S. GDP projections and updated RPA U.S. GDP, personal income, and disposable personal income projections by scenario, 2010-2060 (billion 2006 USD).

	2000	2010	2020	2030	2040	2050	2060
GDP — IPCC							
A1B	10,654	13,456	16,888	21,093	26,112	31,117	38,524
A2	10,282	12,484	14,986	18,061	21,436	24,825	30,330
B2	11,297	14,586	17,017	18,905	21,193	23,466	25,640
GDP — RPA							
A1B	13,195	14,736	19,029	23,424	28,835	35,496	43,696
A2	13,195	13,679	16,890	20,057	23,683	28,313	34,401
B2	13,195	15,974	19,164	20,990	23,416	26,778	29,084
RPA Personal Income							
A1B	10,768	12,073	15,969	19,322	23,785	29,280	36,043
A2	10,768	11,207	13,932	16,544	19,353	23,354	28,376
B2	10,768	13,087	15,808	17,313	19,315	22,088	23,990
RPA Disposable Personal Income							
A1B	9,629	10,796	14,036	17,278	21,269	26,182	32,230
A2	9,629	10,022	12,458	14,794	17,469	20,884	25,374
B2	9,629	11,702	14,136	15,482	17,275	19,751	21,452

USDA Forest Service Gen. Tech. Rep. RMRS-GTR-272. 2012

11

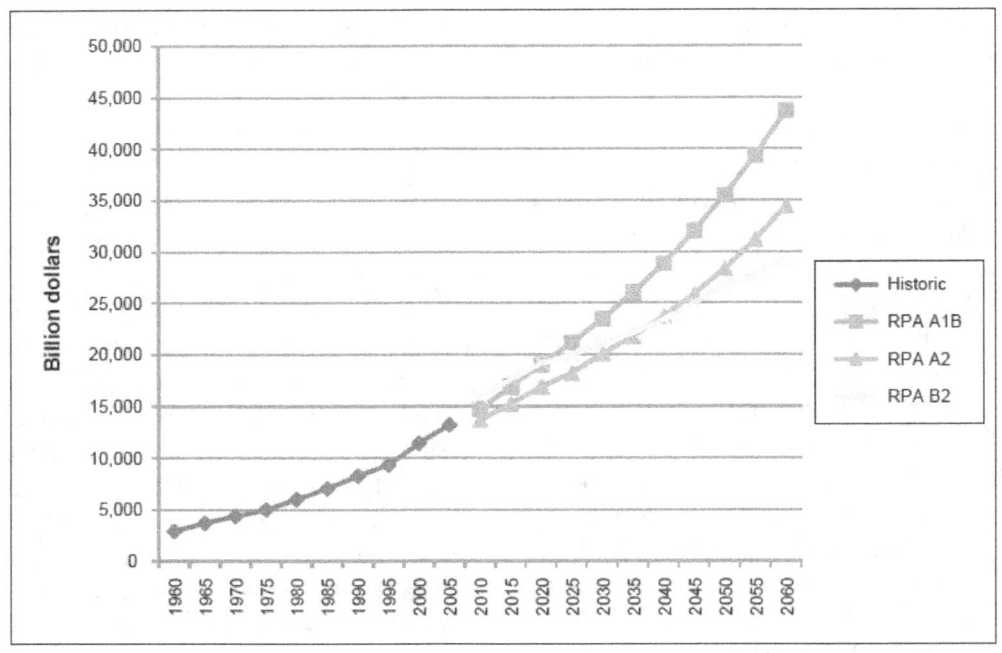

Figure 4—Historic U.S. GDP and projected U.S. GDP to 2060 by RPA scenario.

U.S. income at the county level

The national DPI and PI projections were disaggregated to the county level to facilitate use in the RPA Assessment models. To accomplish this, we first derived per capita PI (PCPI) and per capita DPI (PCDPI) for individual counties based on the Woods & Poole 2006 county level income data and 2006 county population levels. The 2006 county-level PCPI and PCDPI were then multiplied by projected county population to derive a base estimate of total county PI and DPI for the projection period. These base estimates were then adjusted to sum to the projected total national PI and DPI levels described in the previous section. This approach maintains a constant relationship between county per capita measures and the national averages (for example, a county with a PCPI at 90 percent of the national level in 2006 will maintain that 90 percent ratio in 2060), and it assumes a constant ratio of DPI to PI at the per capita and national aggregate levels (in other words the tax rate is constant). At the same time, it assures that all national aggregates equal the estimated income projections described above. These simplifying assumptions allow for a relatively straightforward estimation of county-level income that depends on county-level population projections and national-level income projections.

Issues with updating the U.S. population and economic projections

Population, GDP, and income are important variables in determining GHG emissions levels. Although the U.S. population accounts for a small proportion of the world population, the U.S. contribution to emissions is much higher than its percentage of world population. Therefore, updating the U.S. population and GDP projections could lead to slightly higher global emissions than were projected in the IPCC emissions scenarios. The impact of underestimating the climate forcing captured by the emissions scenarios included in the RPA analyses is unknown. Regardless, we considered re-aligning the IPCC U.S.-level economic and population data with more recent data to be critical for projecting national resource effects within the RPA resource modeling systems. Even if GHG emissions would increase under the adjusted U.S. projections, we assumed that the relative resource impacts between scenarios would not change.

The IPCC emissions scenarios and the adjusted U.S. projections for the 2010 RPA scenarios were completed before the global economic downturn. We chose 2006 as the base year for the U.S. economic variables because they were the most recent data available when the scenarios were constructed. The projection trend line for the United States from 2006 to 2010 does not account for the downturn in GDP and other economic variables through 2010, creating a discontinuity in the early years of the projection period.

Generally, long-term projections are not intended to predict temporary ups and downs, meaning recessions would not be part of the projected trend. However, the global recession was severe with varied recovery around the world, where developing countries have recovered more rapidly than the developed world. The change in focus for the 2010 RPA Assessment from a "most likely" approach to a "scenario" approach provided a more robust set of projections about the range of potential futures. The scenario approach recognizes that the scenarios are not intended to predict a single future. Likewise, economic conditions at present may have few long-run effects on forest conditions or renewable resources. Current conditions should be averaged into the last several years of historical experience, and specific attention to the values foreseen in the next five years is not warranted.

U.S. Bioenergy Projections

We linked assumptions about the role of biomass in bioenergy projections to the IPCC emissions scenarios as we did with other RPA Assessment assumptions discussed in this document. The assumptions for bioenergy projections were input to the RPA Forest Assessment Modeling System that includes the Global Forest Products Model (GFPM) and the U.S. Forest Products Module (USFPM). Our approach accounted for relevant IPCC macro region land use projections as well as regional biomass energy projections provided by IPCC emissions scenarios and their supporting database (Nakicenovic and others 2000). For a detailed explanation of the RPA Assessment bioenergy assumptions, see Ince and others (2011).

The IPCC emissions scenario database provided global land use projections for each of its four major modeling regions (called "macro" regions – see Appendix B). The land use projections associated with the emissions scenarios included several categories of land use that produce biomass for energy, including non-forest biomass energy plantations, agricultural cropland, and forest land. Furthermore, these projections provided changes in land use and biomass energy production for each of the four macro regions, from which we deduced relationships between projected land use and biomass energy production.

In all three emissions scenarios considered in the 2010 RPA Assessment, expansion of biomass energy plantation area projected in the IPCC macro regions was directly correlated with projected regional expansion in primary biomass energy production. Comparing across scenarios, A1B had the largest regional expansion in the area of biomass energy plantations and also biomass energy production, while expansions of biomass energy plantation area and biomass energy production were both smaller in the A2 and B2 scenarios. Also, note that biomass energy plantation area only began to expand by the year 2020 in all scenarios, coinciding with projected regional expansion in biomass energy production, while the area of forest land and cropland in macro regions remained relatively static throughout the projection period in all three scenarios. We deduced that non-forest biomass energy plantations were an important element of biomass energy supply according to emissions scenarios.

Having concluded that non-forest biomass energy plantations, agricultural crops and biomass residues are all important elements of global biomass energy supply along with fuelwood in the RPA scenarios, we applied a direct approach to projecting the expansion of roundwood fuelwood consumption. Specifically, we deducted estimated energy supply from biomass plantations, agricultural crops, and residues from the projected total biomass energy production, yielding a remainder, which was the implicit consumption of roundwood fuelwood.

Toward this end, we first computed projected production and consumption of biomass from non-forest biomass energy plantations based on IPCC projections of regional biomass energy plantation area multiplied by conventional estimates of biomass energy plantation productivity per macro region. Next, we estimated other non-roundwood biomass used for energy consumption, which mainly consisted of biomass from agricultural crops and crop residues, plus other non-roundwood sources, including wood residues. We estimated biomass energy from cropland and residue biomass by macro region for the year 2000 by subtracting the energy equivalent of roundwood fuelwood consumption in the year 2000 from the biomass energy production in the year 2000. We then projected the cropland and residue biomass output based on IPCC projections of cropland area.

USDA Forest Service Gen. Tech. Rep. RMRS-GTR-272. 2012

13

Next we computed global and regional projections of roundwood fuelwood consumption for the three RPA scenarios based on the IPCC projections of biomass energy production with deductions for the projected biomass consumption from all non-fuelwood sources as described above. Roundwood fuelwood consumption estimates were also calibrated to precisely match historical roundwood fuelwood consumption data by macro region as reported by Food and Agricultural Organizations Statistics (FAOSTAT) (on-line FAO forestry database, at http://faostat.fao.org/site/626/default. aspx#ancor). Figure 5 illustrates the estimates of global biomass consumption for energy by RPA scenario.

Using the imputed estimates of roundwood fuelwood consumption, we derived preliminary expansion factors for projecting fuelwood consumption out to 2060 for each macro region and emissions scenario (table 5).

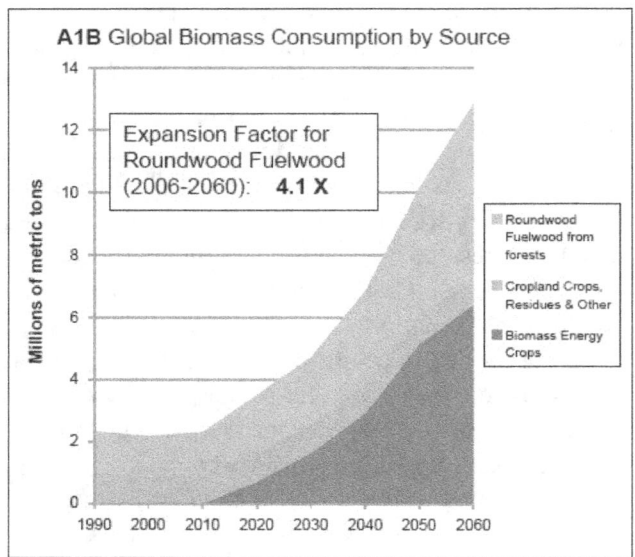

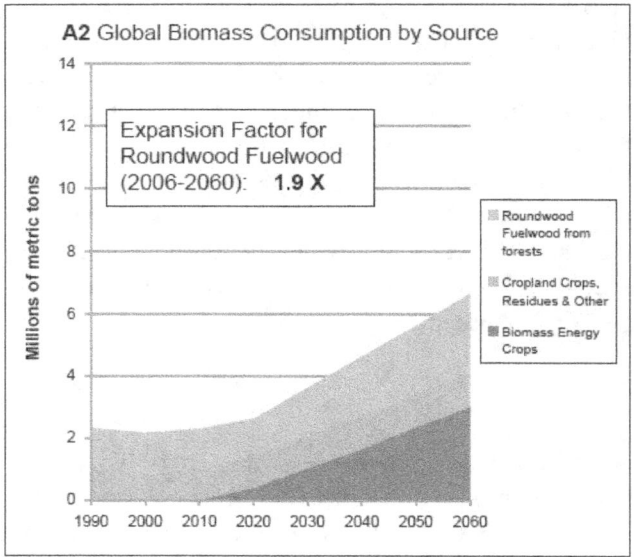

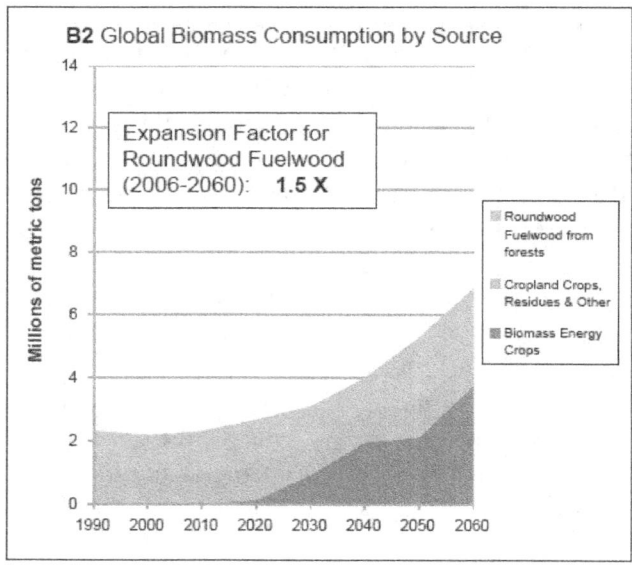

Figure 5—Estimated global biomass consumption for energy (millions of metric tons per year) by source for three RPA scenarios, based on interpretation of IPCC emissions scenario land use projections and other information.

USDA Forest Service Gen. Tech. Rep. RMRS-GTR-272. 2012

Table 5—Preliminary expansion factors and final expansion factor targets for global and IPCC regional roundwood fuelwood consumption for RPA scenarios (2006 to 2060).

	Preliminary	Final Targets
GLOBAL		
A1B (AIM)	4.1 X	4.5 X
A2 (ASF)	1.9 X	2.2 X
B2 (MESSAGE)	1.5 X	2.6 X
OECD 90		
A1B (AIM)	12.8 X	14.0 X
A2 (ASF)	7.4 X	8.1 X
B2 (MESSAGE)	2.6 X	3.0 X
REF		
A1B (AIM)	7.5 X	7.5 X
A2 (ASF)	4.2 X	4.2 X
B2 (MESSAGE)	3.7 X	3.7 X
ASIA		
A1B (AIM)	1.7 X	1.7 X
A2 (ASF)	0.9 X	0.9 X
B2 (MESSAGE)	1.6 X	1.6 X
ALM		
A1B AIM)	4.8 X	4.8 X
A2 (A2 ASF)	1.8 X	1.8 X
B2 (MESSAGE)	3.4 X	3.4 X

Secondly, we also applied common regional elasticities of fuelwood demand with respect to the demand growth rates to calibrate the model solution. The final target expansion factors for fuelwood consumption in each country within each macro region were computed by multiplying the preliminary expansion factor for the region times the country's share of regional GDP in 2060, divided by the country's share of regional fuelwood consumption in 2006. Compound growth rates for fuelwood demand in each country were computed on the basis of the expansion factors for each country. This procedure ensured that target expansion factors for fuelwood consumption in each country were calibrated to each country's regional share of GDP in 2060, while regional totals were also calibrated to the imputed regional shares of fuelwood consumption derived from emissions scenarios.

This approach resulted in projected U.S. and OECD90 region (see Appendix B) roundwood fuelwood consumption expanding at a rate that was higher than the global average rate of expansion. This is partly because the fuelwood expansion factors for the OECD90 region are higher than other regions for two of the three scenarios, and because the U.S. share of roundwood fuelwood consumption in the OECD90 region was only 12 percent in 2006, but the projected U.S. shares of regional GDP in 2060 are much higher (42 percent in the A1B scenario, 44 percent in the A2 scenario, and 49 percent in the B2 scenario). Thus, the U.S. share of regional fuelwood consumption had to increase to match U.S. regional GDP shares in 2060. In addition, the United States has a fairly abundant wood supply, which also helps to support expansion in U.S. fuelwood consumption relative to other countries and regions.

For the United States and for many other countries the resulting rates of expansion in wood energy consumption are prodigious in all RPA scenarios, and by far the highest in the A1B scenario, followed by the A2 scenario, and lowest in the B2 scenario (figure 6). In the A1B scenario, for example, U.S. wood fuel feedstock[4] consumption climbs to levels that dwarf U.S. consumption of wood for all other end uses (about five times higher by 2060 than all other wood uses) while in the B2 scenario U.S. wood fuel feedstock consumption climbs to a level just slightly higher than all other commercial uses. Although the projected rates of expansion in wood energy consumption are higher in the United States than worldwide (figure 6), global wood fuel consumption quantity is currently much higher than in the United States (especially in developing countries), and wood energy consumption in the rest of the world remains quantitatively higher than U.S. consumption throughout the projection period in all scenarios.

---

[4] U.S. wood fuel feedstock includes conventional fuelwood harvest, as well as other wood materials projected to be used for energy that have not been used historically (harvest residues, pulpwood roundwood, fiber resides, and sawlogs). See Ince and others (2011) for more details.

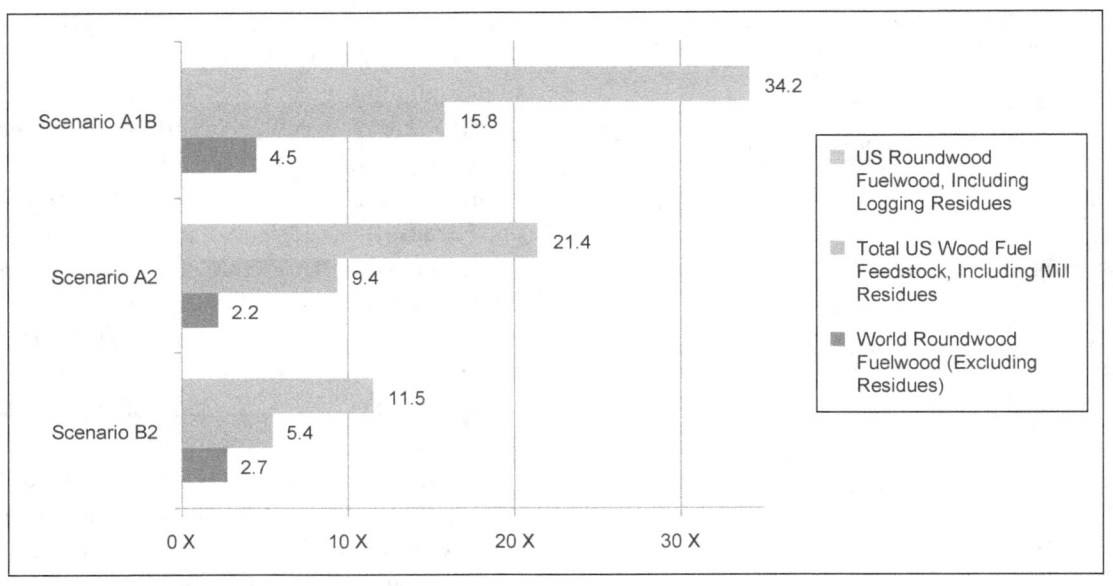

Figure 6—Projected expansion factors from 2006 to 2060 in the volumes of wood consumed for energy by RPA scenario, including total U.S. wood fuel feedstock consumption, U.S. roundwood fuelwood consumption, and world roundwood fuelwood consumption.

U.S. Land Use Projections

Land use change is a major driver and manifestation of resource change (for example, Alig and Butler 2004, Lubowski and others 2006). These changes are responsive to changes in population and economic growth, and in turn, they interact with the conditions and trends of renewable resources. Land use change analyses provide a critical link to other models that analyze resource changes, such as wildlife habitat and timber availability.

Land use projections were used as an independent variable in several of the resource analyses for the 2010 RPA Assessment. The IPCC emissions scenarios included projections of forestland area for the world and the OECD90 region. However, we decided not to link our land use projections to the IPCC projections directly because data were not available at the country level. The United States has land use data that can be used as a starting point for projections that provides a better basis for the analysis. The land use model includes both population and income variables that came from the county-level population and income projections described earlier, so the RPA land use projections are linked to the IPCC scenarios through those variables. The land use projections are documented in more detail in Wear (2011). We were unable to incorporate climate effects into the land use change models for the RPA Assessment. Depending on the changes in projected temperature and precipitation, it is possible that agriculture and forestry production possibilities may change in some regions. Consistent county-level data on potential changes in productivity and/or associated returns to rural land uses as a result of climate across the United States were not available to facilitate such analyses.

We projected land use distributions at the county level for all counties in the conterminous United States using econometric models to fit to historical data. Separate models were developed for the four RPA Assessment regions (figure 2) with two exceptions. Texas and Oklahoma were split between regions, with the forested eastern portions of each state included in the South's model and the remainder in the Rocky Mountain model. For model estimation then, Texas and Oklahoma counties were included with regions with most similar conditions, but for all reporting we aggregate all of Texas and Oklahoma into the South, consistent with the RPA Assessment regions shown in figure 2.

The land use model had two major components. The first used county-level population changes and personal income to simulate future urbanization, because urban uses were assumed to be the dominant land type in all land use conversions (in other words land is converted to urban, but urban is not converted to other land uses). The second component allocated the remaining rural land among competing uses based on economic returns to the various rural land uses.

The econometric models were fit to land use change data from 1987 and 1997 to ensure the projected land use changes were generally consistent with observed urbanization intensities and rural land use changes. We held constant the real rents of both agricultural and forest land uses—in effect assuming that the relative returns to these uses remains constant through the forecast period. Historical land use data were derived from the National Resources Inventory (NRI) survey of land uses conducted for the years 1987 and 1997. The NRI provides the only consistent, repeated, and exhaustive measure of nonfederal land in the United States. Unfortunately, 1997 was the last year for which the detailed county-level data were made available. We used NRI county estimates of the areas of nonfederal land in pasture, cropland, forest, range, and urban uses. All land use change occurs within this "mutable" land base; all other uses are held constant over the projection period, including federal land, water area, enrolled Conservation Reserve Program lands, and utility corridors (table 6).

Table 6A—U.S. major land use projections for RPA scenario A1B by RPA region, 1997-2060.

RPA Region	Year	Land Use Category					Total Area
		Urban	Cropland	Forest	Pasture	Range	
		- - - - - - - - - - - - - - - Thousand acres - - - - - - - - - - - - - - -					
North							
	1997	28,929	142,190	149,747	36,063	86	357,015
	2010	33,445	140,183	147,763	35,538	86	357,015
	2020	37,590	138,350	145,928	35,060	86	357,015
	2030	41,316	136,706	144,267	34,640	86	357,015
	2040	45,488	134,857	142,413	34,171	86	357,015
	2050	50,172	132,771	140,338	33,648	86	357,015
	2060	55,441	130,417	138,007	33,064	86	357,015
Pacific Coast							
	1997	6,997	19,770	38,433	4,115	32,983	102,298
	2010	8,736	19,414	37,736	4,030	32,382	102,298
	2020	9,880	19,182	37,262	3,975	31,999	102,298
	2030	10,958	18,962	36,813	3,923	31,642	102,298
	2040	12,109	18,727	36,331	3,870	31,261	102,298
	2050	13,339	18,476	35,818	3,814	30,850	102,298
	2060	14,662	18,206	35,267	3,756	30,406	102,298
Rocky Mountain							
	1997	6,851	123,385	28,744	15,596	256,332	430,907
	2010	9,138	122,728	28,484	15,467	255,091	430,907
	2020	10,694	122,267	28,302	15,382	254,261	430,907
	2030	12,154	121,845	28,127	15,303	253,477	430,907
	2040	13,727	121,386	27,952	15,218	252,623	430,907
	2050	15,475	120,874	27,761	15,128	251,669	430,907
	2060	17,375	120,299	27,556	15,032	250,645	430,907
South							
	1997	29,879	84,292	175,812	61,191	111,854	463,029
	2010	38,368	81,736	171,837	60,109	110,979	463,029
	2020	44,923	79,842	168,482	59,285	110,497	463,029
	2030	50,770	78,213	165,481	58,497	110,068	463,029
	2040	57,083	76,462	162,178	57,701	109,606	463,029
	2050	63,966	74,563	158,544	56,831	109,124	463,029
	2060	71,630	72,498	154,434	55,863	108,604	463,029
Total							
	1997	72,656	369,637	392,736	116,965	401,255	1,353,249
	2010	89,687	364,061	385,820	115,144	398,538	1,353,249
	2020	103,087	359,641	379,974	113,702	396,843	1,353,249
	2030	115,198	355,726	374,688	112,363	395,273	1,353,249
	2040	128,407	351,432	368,874	110,960	393,576	1,353,249
	2050	142,952	346,684	362,461	109,421	391,729	1,353,249
	2060	159,108	341,420	355,264	107,715	389,741	1,353,249

USDA Forest Service Gen. Tech. Rep. RMRS-GTR-272. 2012

17

Table 6B—U.S. major land use projections for RPA scenario A2 by RPA region, 1997-2060.

RPA Region	Year	Land Use Category					Total Area
		Urban	Cropland	Forest	Pasture	Range	
		- - - - - - - - - - - - - - Thousand acres - - - - - - - - - - - - - -					
North							
	1997	28,929	142,190	149,747	36,063	86	357,015
	2010	32,704	140,549	148,053	35,623	86	357,015
	2020	36,105	139,072	146,524	35,228	86	357,015
	2030	39,140	137,762	145,143	34,884	86	357,015
	2040	42,375	136,363	143,673	34,518	86	357,015
	2050	46,182	134,710	141,945	34,091	86	357,015
	2060	50,687	132,750	139,897	33,595	86	357,015
Pacific Coast							
	1997	6,997	19,770	38,433	4,115	32,983	102,298
	2010	8,741	19,409	37,735	4,029	32,384	102,298
	2020	9,858	19,178	37,270	3,974	32,017	102,298
	2030	10,930	18,955	36,821	3,923	31,669	102,298
	2040	12,081	18,715	36,336	3,869	31,297	102,298
	2050	13,397	18,440	35,782	3,809	30,870	102,298
	2060	14,928	18,119	35,137	3,742	30,372	102,298
Rocky Mountain							
	1997	6,851	123,385	28,744	15,596	256,332	430,907
	2010	8,981	122,805	28,491	15,476	255,155	430,907
	2020	10,383	122,419	28,316	15,400	254,388	430,907
	2030	11,706	122,071	28,149	15,329	253,652	430,907
	2040	13,107	121,709	27,981	15,254	252,856	430,907
	2050	14,644	121,297	27,798	15,177	251,991	430,907
	2060	16,500	120,802	27,578	15,085	250,942	430,907
South							
	1997	29,879	84,292	175,812	61,191	111,854	463,029
	2010	37,852	81,753	172,413	60,489	110,993	463,029
	2020	43,710	79,989	169,675	59,576	110,549	463,029
	2030	48,709	78,651	167,252	58,748	110,140	463,029
	2040	53,837	77,287	164,747	57,913	109,716	463,029
	2050	59,699	75,747	161,861	56,953	109,240	463,029
	2060	66,452	73,975	158,498	55,889	108,686	463,029
Total							
	1997	72,656	369,637	392,736	116,965	401,255	1,353,249
	2010	88,278	364,516	386,692	115,617	398,618	1,353,249
	2020	100,056	360,658	381,785	114,178	397,040	1,353,249
	2030	110,485	357,439	377,365	112,884	395,547	1,353,249
	2040	121,400	354,074	372,737	111,554	393,955	1,353,249
	2050	133,922	350,194	367,386	110,030	392,187	1,353,249
	2060	148,567	345,646	361,110	108,311	390,086	1,353,249

Table 6C—U.S. major land use projections for RPA scenario B2 by RPA region, 1997-2060.

RPA Region	Year	Land Use Category Urban	Cropland	Forest	Pasture	Range	Total Area
		---------------- Thousand acres ----------------					
North							
	1997	28,929	142,190	149,747	36,063	86	357,015
	2010	34,555	139,669	147,290	35,416	86	357,015
	2020	37,662	138,310	145,906	35,051	86	357,015
	2030	39,237	137,630	145,199	34,863	86	357,015
	2040	41,135	136,789	144,367	34,638	86	357,015
	2050	43,695	135,652	143,238	34,344	86	357,015
	2060	45,437	134,901	142,450	34,142	86	357,015
Pacific Coast							
	1997	6,997	19,770	38,433	4,115	32,983	102,298
	2010	8,859	19,393	37,687	4,025	32,334	102,298
	2020	9,860	19,186	37,270	3,976	32,006	102,298
	2030	10,528	19,045	36,985	3,942	31,797	102,298
	2040	11,158	18,913	36,716	3,911	31,601	102,298
	2050	11,911	18,755	36,397	3,876	31,359	102,298
	2060	12,590	18,608	36,108	3,844	31,147	102,298
Rocky Mountain							
	1997	6,851	123,385	28,744	15,596	256,332	430,907
	2010	9,411	122,617	28,462	15,451	254,966	430,907
	2020	10,699	122,260	28,304	15,382	254,263	430,907
	2030	11,536	122,060	28,192	15,337	253,783	430,907
	2040	12,424	121,828	28,084	15,291	253,281	430,907
	2050	13,512	121,529	27,960	15,235	252,671	430,907
	2060	14,438	121,312	27,846	15,190	252,121	430,907
South							
	1997	29,879	84,292	175,812	61,191	111,854	463,029
	2010	40,288	80,986	170,996	60,315	110,915	463,029
	2020	45,768	79,338	168,435	59,459	110,499	463,029
	2030	48,739	78,604	167,025	58,892	110,242	463,029
	2040	52,043	77,754	165,351	58,365	109,987	463,029
	2050	56,234	76,644	163,196	57,743	109,683	463,029
	2060	59,318	75,864	161,660	57,232	109,426	463,029
Total							
	1997	72,656	369,637	392,736	116,965	401,255	1,353,249
	2010	93,113	362,665	384,435	115,207	398,301	1,353,249
	2020	103,989	359,094	379,915	113,868	396,854	1,353,249
	2030	110,040	357,339	377,401	113,034	395,908	1,353,249
	2040	116,760	355,284	374,518	112,205	394,955	1,353,249
	2050	125,352	352,580	370,791	111,198	393,799	1,353,249
	2060	131,783	350,685	368,064	110,408	392,780	1,353,249

USDA Forest Service Gen. Tech. Rep. RMRS-GTR-272. 2012

19

Patterns of rural uses reflect biome boundaries (e.g., natural boundaries between grassland and forestland) and productivity determined by biophysical conditions along with comparative advantages for producing various goods and services determined by cost and return attributes. Forest uses dominate the South, the Northeast, the Lake States and the Pacific Northwest. Cropland is concentrated in the Plains and Midwest, while rangeland is concentrated in the High Plains and Intermountain West. Urban land, the least abundant land use, corresponds with the nation's cities, and the largest area of pastureland is found at the boundary between grassland and forest biomes from eastern Texas to northern Missouri.

The changes in major land uses over the projection period for scenario A1B are summarized in figure 7. The pattern of change is similar for the other scenarios, but the change in acres is smaller in both A2 and B2. Scenario A1B, with an intermediate level of population growth but strong growth in personal income, yields the highest rate of urbanization, while scenario B2 has the lowest. The total area of urbanization is similar across the three scenarios until 2040, after which urbanization diverges more strongly across scenarios, generally reflecting the increased divergence in population and income growth across scenarios in the later decades of the projection period. The total area of urban land increases the most in the South, followed by the North. However, the rate of increase in urban land is highest in the Rocky Mountain region.

In all scenarios, only urban land area increases over the projection period, while all other land uses experience losses. Forest losses vary regionally. The South has the largest loss of forest, reflecting both an abundant forest resource and the region with the highest projected population growth and urbanization (figure 8). The North has the second greatest loss of forest land. Because the majority of forest land in the West is public, and therefore held fixed, the projected change in forest area for the western regions is relatively small. Cropland losses are greatest in the eastern United States, while rangeland losses are concentrated in the Rocky Mountain region.

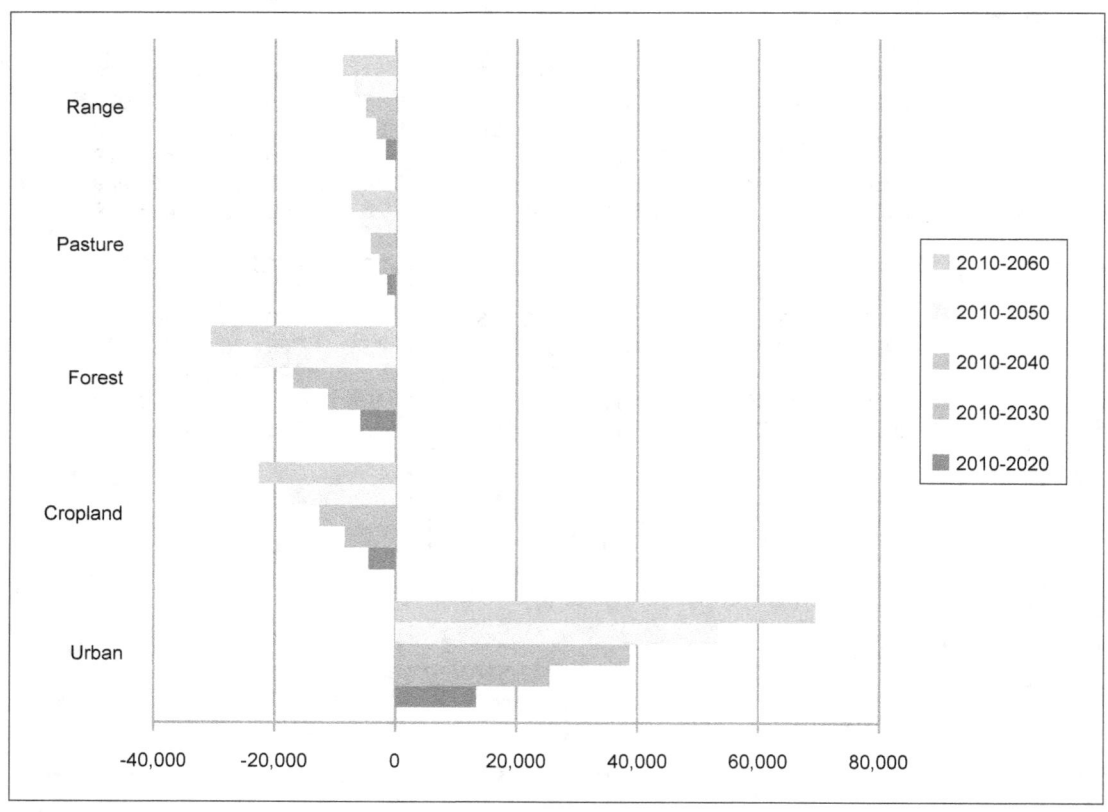

Figure 7—Projected cumulative change in the areas of major nonfederal land uses in conterminous United States for RPA scenario A1B (thousand acres).

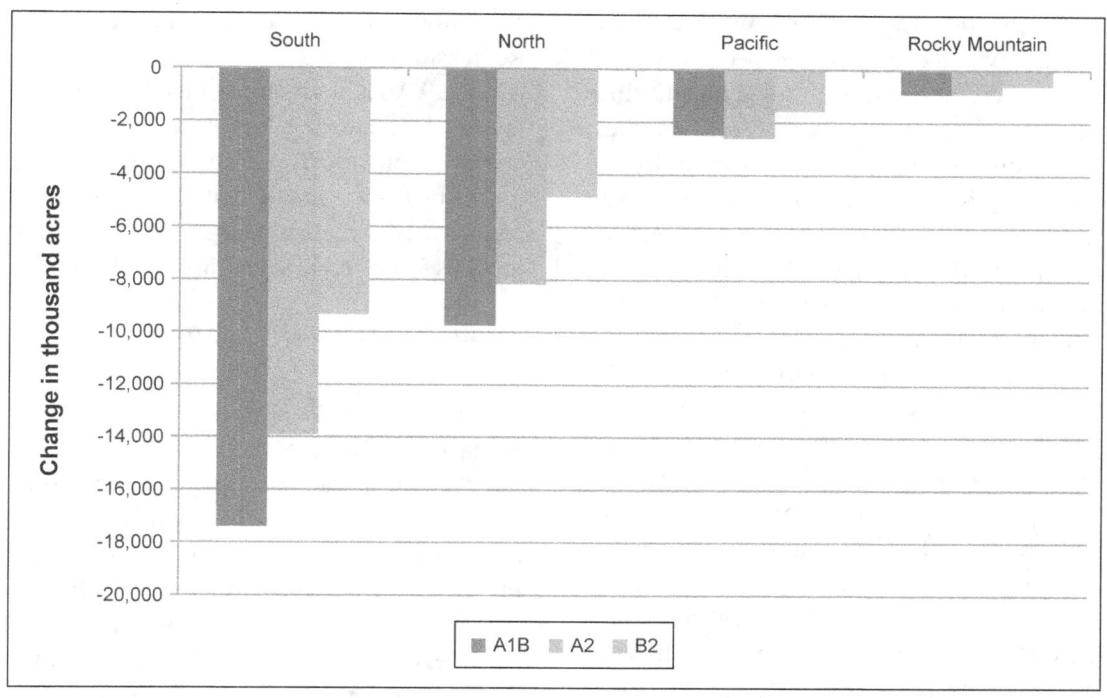

Figure 8—Change in conterminous U.S. nonfederal forest area from 2010-2060 by RPA Assessment region and RPA scenario (thousand acres).

U.S. Climate Projections

Global climate projections – from emissions scenarios to future climate

In order to determine how emissions influence atmospheric chemistry and consequently the climate, emissions from the IAMs were converted to atmospheric concentrations of carbon dioxide. Two different carbon cycle models (ISAM and Bern-CC) were used to model the dynamics of the global carbon cycle, and determine, given the carbon dioxide emissions, the future atmospheric CO_2 concentrations (Prentice and others 2001). These projections of atmospheric concentrations of carbon dioxide and other GHGs (Ebhalt and others 2001) are used to alter the atmospheric chemistry in the GCMs so that the effects of GHG climate forcing on the global climate can be quantified (Meehl and others 2007b). The atmospheric concentrations of carbon dioxide associated with each emissions scenario based on the carbon cycle models are found at http://www.ipcc-data.org/ddc_co2.html. As mentioned previously, global climate projections from the many GCMs using

these emissions scenarios have been archived: for the TAR at the IPCC Data Distribution Centre (DDC); for the AR4, at the Climate Model Intercomparison Project (CMIP3) website. Climate models used in AR4 differed from the climate models used in the three previous IPCC reports and represent many improvements in describing climate processes (Le Treut and others 2007).

Downscaling the IPCC global climate projections

The resolution of GCM global projections stored in either the IPCC DDC or at the CMIP3 website range from 250 to 600 km on the side of the grid, far coarser than that typically used in many impact assessments including the RPA Assessment. Because of the spatial scale of the socio-economic data (U.S. county), most analyses in the RPA Assessment are being conducted at that spatial scale. Hence this necessitated climate projection data at that spatial scale. The development of downscaled climate data is an active area of research that attempts to meet the needs of the climate impact community by providing finer scale climate projections

USDA Forest Service Gen. Tech. Rep. RMRS-GTR-272. 2012

21

(Fowler and others 2007, Hayhoe 2007, Wilby and others 2004). A variety of techniques have been developed to "downscale" the global climate projections to finer spatial scales associated with climate impact studies. Because the techniques introduce some variability, we needed consistency in the downscaling of the climate projections for the RPA Assessment. More detailed documentation of the development of the RPA climate projections and downscaling process can be found in Joyce and others (in review).

We used the delta or change factor method for the downscaling technique, which has been adopted for interpolating both climate observations and climate model output to fine spatial resolutions over large regions (Hamlet and Lettenmaier 1999, Miller and others 2003, Price and others 2004, Ray and others 2010). Monthly time-series data for the conterminous United States and Alaska were obtained for specific realizations (runs) from each GCM, representing both the simulated 20th century (20C3M realizations for the 1961–2000 period) and the selected emissions scenarios A1B, A2, and B2 for the 21st century (2001-2100). The change factor at each GCM grid node was computed by either subtracting from (projected temperature variables) or dividing by (other projected climate variables) the mean of that month's values for the simulated historical period. We used the historical period 1961–1990 as the baseline. The simulated historical GCM data was available for this period as were observed historical climate data. The global grid change factor data were spatially interpolated. ANUSPLIN was used to fit a two-dimensional spline "surface" function uniquely to each month's data (deltas) for each of the six normalized climate variables (ANUSPLIN, developed by M Hutchinson and colleagues at Australian National University in Canberra (http://cres.anu.edu.au/outputs/anusplin.php; see also McKenney and others 2006). The fitted spline functions were, in turn, used to create gridded data sets for each monthly variable covering North America at a spatial resolution of standard 5 arc-minute spatial resolution (0.0833 degree ≈ 10 km at mid-latitudes) using latitude and longitude as independent variables.

Because climate models typically have very low horizontal resolution, their representation of topographic effects on local climate is necessarily poor. For this reason, the normalized and interpolated climate model data (delta values) were combined with climatological data for the reference period interpolated to the same resolution, using data from the Parameter-elevation Regressions on Independent Slopes Model (PRISM) (Daly 1994). The normalization (computation of the change factors), the interpolation procedures, and the use of observed historical climatology effectively removed model biases associated with the global model means and allowed direct comparison of the downscaled projections for different scenarios and different GCM runs.

Climate projections for the U.S. at the 5 arc-minute grid and U.S. county level

Four climate variables were downscaled for the RPA scenarios using the PRISM historical climatology: monthly mean daily maximum temperature, monthly mean daily minimum temperature, monthly precipitation, and monthly mean daily potential evapotranspiration. The mean annual temperature for all scenarios increases at the scale of the conterminous United States over the next 100 years from the historical mean of 10.86 degrees C to a range of 14.65 degrees C for the B2 scenario, 14.94 degrees C for the A1B scenario, and 15.95 degrees C for the A2 scenario. Each scenario summary represents the mean of the three climate models used in this study for each scenario. While A2 shows the greatest surface warming by 2100, the relative degrees of warming vary over the projection period (Joyce and others, in review.). For example, at 2060, the A1B scenario shows the greatest increase in the mean annual temperature (figure 9). The warming trends are similar across the scenarios until 2060 when the scenario temperatures begin to depart from each other. While the climate projections extend to 2100, the RPA Assessment resource analyses stop at 2060.

For the 2010 RPA Assessment projection period, the A1B scenario mean represents the warmest and driest scenario at the scale of the United States (figure 9). The A2 scenario becomes the wettest, although the precipitation changes at the scale of the U.S. are small at 2060. Regional differences in precipitation projections vary greatly. The B2 scenario projects the least warming of these three scenarios. The individual model projections vary across the individual scenario. For example, within the A2 scenario, the CGCM3.1 model projects the least warming and the MIROC3.2 model projects the greatest warming within this scenario (Joyce and others, in review).

For purposes of the RPA Assessment, county delineation is critical. We used the Forest Inventory and

22

USDA Forest Service Gen. Tech. Rep. RMRS-GTR-272. 2012

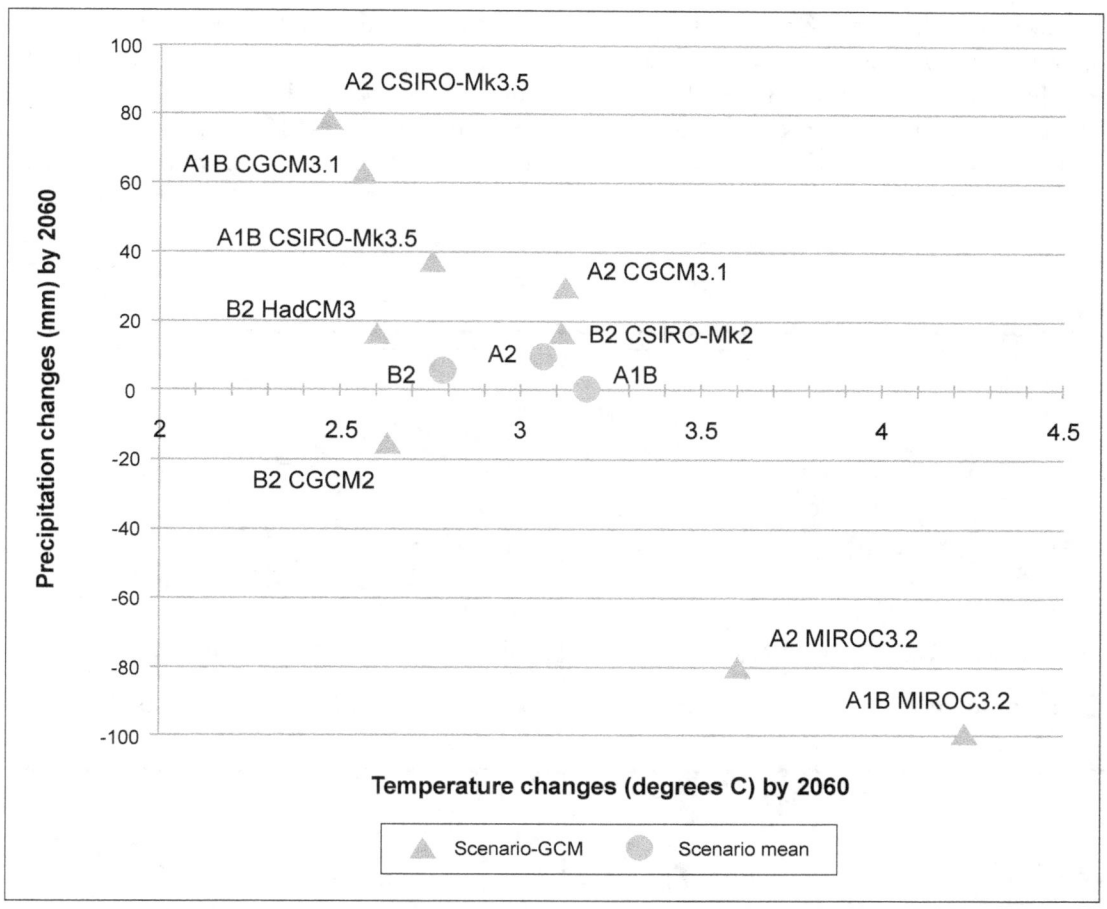

Figure 9—U.S. temperature and precipitation changes from the historical period (1961-1990) to the decade surrounding the year 2060 (2055-2064). The scenario-GCM pairs are defined in table 2.

Analysis (FIA) Survey Unit and County Coverage as the GIS delineation for counties. An overlay file between the 5 arc-minute grid and the County boundaries was developed in ArcGIS 9.2. This resulting layer was merged with the projected climate data. Once merged, the county means for the climate variables were calculated using a weighted mean value of the underlying 5 arc-minute grids within the county. With the overlay of the county shape file on the grid shape file, some grids are assigned to more than one county. During the overlay process the area of each grid falling wholly or partially within the county was calculated. These areas were used as weights to calculate the county means for respective climate variables. Note that to obtain state or U.S. temperature and precipitation values, the county or the grid data should be area-weighted in those calculations, as county sizes vary greatly across the United States.

Summary

The RPA Assessment provides a nationally consistent analysis of the status and trends of the Nation's renewable resources. Variability in data sources and models provide a considerable challenge in developing a coherent framework across multiple resource analyses. The set of underlying assumptions described in this document are used to ensure consistency across RPA Assessment analyses.

We chose to take a scenario approach for the 2010 RPA Assessment to provide a shared view of potential futures. We linked our scenarios to the emissions scenarios and global climate projections used in the IPCC TAR and AR4 to recognize the influence of global forces on domestic resource conditions and trends. We

USDA Forest Service Gen. Tech. Rep. RMRS-GTR-272. 2012

23

originally intended to include four IPCC-based scenarios, but the availability of global climate projections at the time limited selections within the A1 family. Therefore, we chose to develop future scenarios linked to IPCC scenarios A1B, A2, and B2.

Figure 10 portrays the variation in the common assumptions across the three RPA scenarios. Population and income grow under all three scenarios, although at varying rates. The A1B scenario has the highest economic growth rate, coupled with a moderate population

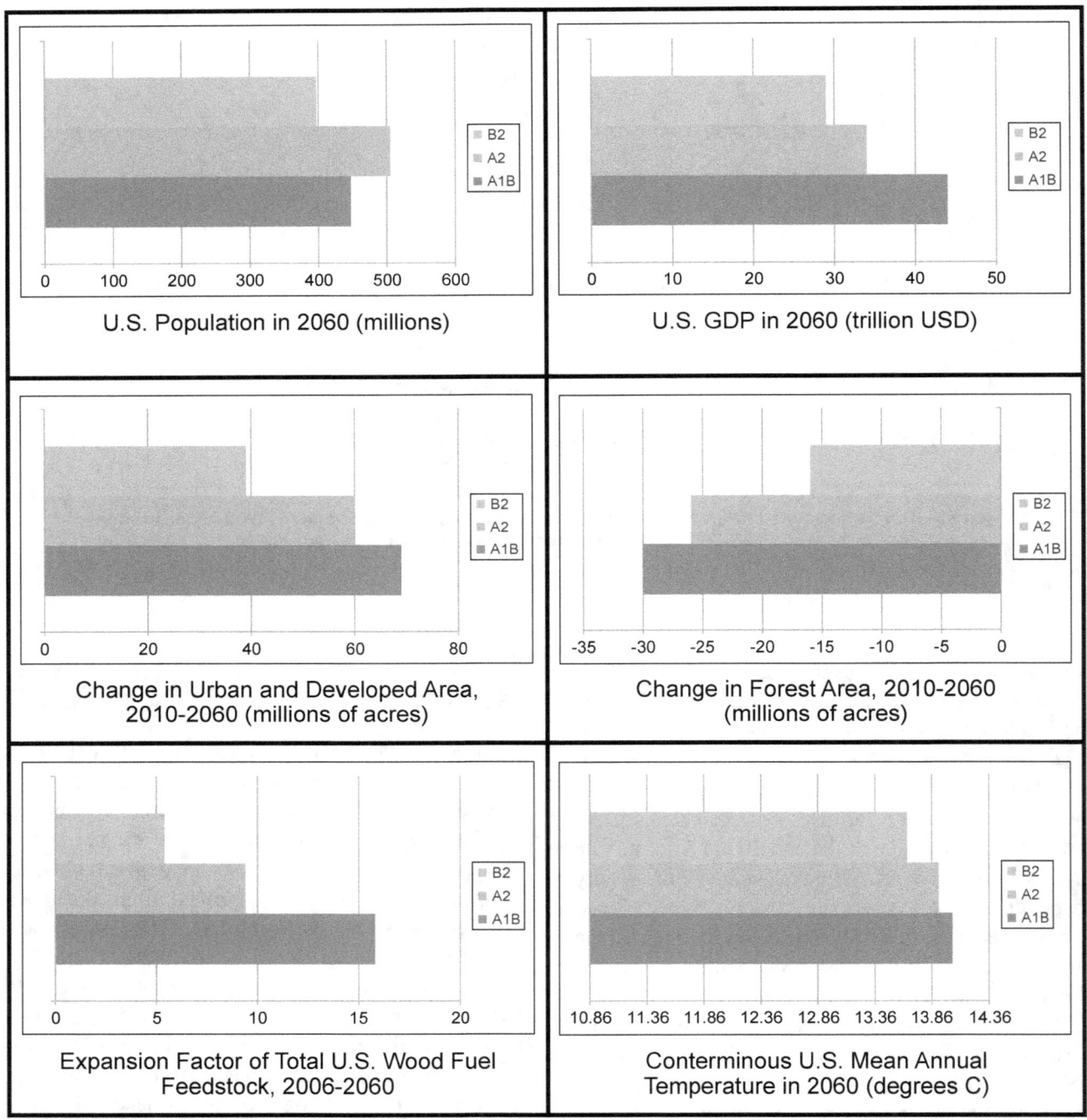

Figure 10—Summary of variation in assumptions across RPA scenarios.

projection. Economic growth had more influence than population growth in projections of land use change: scenario A1B had the greatest rate of change, followed by A2, even though A2 has the greatest growth in U.S. population. Similarly, A1B had the greatest projected increase in use of biomass for bioenergy. Mean annual temperature increases under all three scenarios in the conterminous United States. Scenario A1B shows the greatest warming to 2060, although by 2100 (the time frame for IPCC projections), A2 has the greatest surface warming. Scenario B2 results are consistently lower than the other two scenarios, reflecting lower population growth. Even though economic growth is relatively low in B2, per capita income for B2 exceeds per capita income for A2 by 2060.

The RPA scenarios and the associated socioeconomic and climate projections described in this document were used in various natural resource models to project a range of futures for water yield and water use, forest inventory and wood markets, wildlife habitat, recreation use, and other resources. Those results will be summarized in the forthcoming RPA Assessment summary, with more detailed information in a series of supporting technical publications.

Literature Cited

Alcamo, J.; Ash, N.J.; Butler, C.D.; and others. 2003. Ecosystems and human well-being. Washington, DC: Island Press. 245 p.

Alig, Ralph J.; Butler, Brett J. 2004. Projecting large-scale area changes in land use and land cover for terrestrial carbon analyses. Environmental Management 33(4): 443-456.

Bachelet, D.; Lenihan, J.; Drapek, R.; Neilson, R.P. 2008. VEMAP vs. VINCERA: a DGVM sensitivity to differences in climate scenarios. Global and Planetary Change 64: 38-48.

Carpenter, S.R.; Pingali, P.L.; Bennett, E.M.; Zurek, M.B., eds. 2005. Ecosystems and human well-being: scenarios, volume 2. Findings of the scenarios working group of the Millennium Ecosystem Assessment. Washington, DC: Island Press. 560 p.

Daly, C. 1994. A statistical-topographic model for mapping climatological precipitation over mountainous terrain. Journal of Applied Meteorology 33: 140-158.

Ebhalt, D.; Prather, M.; Dentener, F.; Derwent, and others. 2001. Atmospheric chemistry and greenhouse gases. In: Houghton, J.T.; Ding, Y.; Griggs, D.J.; Noguer, M.; van der Linden, P.J.; Dai, X.; Maskell, K.; Johnson, C.A., eds. Climate change 2001: the scientific basis. Contribution of Working Group I to the Third Assessment Report of the Intergovernmental Panel on Climate Change. Cambridge, United Kingdom, and New York: Cambridge University Press 881 p.

Fowler, H.J.; Blenkinsop, S.; Tebaldi, C. 2007. Linking climate change modeling to impacts studies: recent advances in downscaling techniques for hydrological modeling. International Journal of Climatology 27: 1547-1578.

Hamlet, Alan F.; Lettenmaier, Dennis P. 1999. Effects of climate change on hydrology and water resources in the Columbia River Basin. Journal of the American Water Resources Association 35(6): 1597-1623.

Hayhoe, K.; Wake, C.P.; Huntington, T.G.; and others. 2007. Past and future changes in climate and hydrological indicators in the U.S. Northeast. Climate Dynamics 28: 381-407.

Ince, P.J.; Kramp, A.D.; Skog, K.E.; Spelter, H.N.; Wear, D.N. 2011. U.S. Forest Products Module for RPA forest assessment. Res. Pap. FPL-RP-662. Madison, Wisconsin: U.S. Department of Agriculture, Forest Service, Forest Products Laboratory. 61 p.

Intergovernmental Panel on Climate Change [IPCC]. 2007. Climate change 2007: Synthesis Report. Contribution of Working Groups I, II and III to the Fourth AssessmentReport of the Intergovernmental Panel on Climate Change [Core Writing Team, Pachauri, R.K and Reisinger, A.(eds.)]. Geneva, Switzerland: IPCC. 104 p. Available at: http://www.ipcc.ch/publications_and_data/publications_ipcc_fourth_assessment_report_synthesis_report.htm.

Joyce, Linda A., ed. 1995. Productivity of America's forest and climate change. Gen. Tech. Rep. RM-271. Fort Collins, Colorado: U.S. Department of Agriculture, Forest Service, Rocky Mountain Forest and Range Experiment Station. 70 p.

Joyce, Linda A, Birdsey, Richard, tech. eds. 2000. The impact of climate change on America's forests: a technical document supporting the 2000 USDA Forest Service RPA Assessment. Gen. Tech. Rep. RMRS-GTR-59. Fort Collins, Colorado: U.S. Department of Agriculture, Forest Service, Rocky Mountain Forest and Range Experiment Station. 133 p.

Joyce, Linda A.; Fosberg, Michael A.; Comanor, Joan A. 1990. Climate change and America's forests. Gen. Tech. Rept. RM-187. Fort Collins, Colorado: U.S. Department of Agriculture, Forest Service, Rocky Mountain Forest and Range Experiment Station. 12 p.

Joyce, Linda A.; Price, David T.; Coulson, David P.; McKenney, Daniel W.; Siltanen, R. Martin; Papadopol, Pia; Lawrence, Kevin. In review. Projecting climate change in the United States: a technical document supporting the Forest Service 2010 RPA Assessment. Gen. Tech. Rep. Fort Collins, Colorado: U.S. Department of Agriculture, Forest Service, Rocky Mountain Research Station.

Le Treut, H.; Somerville, R.; Cubasch, U.; Ding, Y.; Mauritzen, C.; Mokssit, A.; Peterson,T.; Prather, M. 2007. Historical overview of climate change. In: Solomon, S.; Qin, D.; Manning, M.; Chen, Z.; Marquis, M.; Averyt, K.B.; Tignor M.; Miller, H.L., eds. Climate change 2007: the physical science basis. Contribution of Working Group I to the Fourth Assessment Report of the Intergovernmental Panel on Climate Change. Cambridge, United Kingdom and New York: Cambridge University Press.

Lubowski, R.N.; Plantinga, A.; Stavins, R. 2006. Land-use change and carbon sinks: econometric estimation of the carbon sequestration supply function. Journal of Environmental Economics and Management 51: 135-152.

McKenney, D.; Price, D.; Papadapol, P.; Siltanen, M; Lawrence, K. 2006. High-resolution climate change scenarios for North America. Frontline Technical Note 107. Sault Ste. Marie, Ontario: Canadian Forestry Service, Great Lakes Forestry Centre.

Meehl, G.A.; Covey, C.; Delworth, T.; Latif, M.; McAvaney, B.; Mitchell, J.F.B.; Stouffer, R.J.; Taylor, K.E. 2007a. The WCRP CMIP3 multimodel data set. Bulletin of the American Meteorological Society September 2007: 1383-1394.

Meehl, G.A.; Stocker, T.F.; Collins, W.D.; and others. 2007b. Global climate projections. In: Solomon, S.; Qin, D.; Manning, M.; Chen, Z.; Marquis, M.; Averyt, K.B.; Tignor M.; Miller, H.L., eds. Climate change 2007: the physical science basis. Contribution of Working Group I to the Fourth Assessment Report of the Intergovernmental Panel on Climate Change. Cambridge, United Kingdom and New York: Cambridge University Press.

USDA Forest Service Gen. Tech. Rep. RMRS-GTR-272. 2012

25

Miller, Norman L.; Bashford, Kathy E.; Strem, Eric. 2003. Potential impacts of climate change on California hydrology. Journal of the American Water Resources Association 39(4):771-784.

Nakićenović, N.; Alcamo, J.; Davis, G.; and others. 2000. Emissions scenarios: a special report of Working Group III of the Intergovernmental Panel on Climate Change. Cambridge, United Kingdom and New York: Cambridge University Press. 599 p. Available at: http://www.grida.no/climate/ipcc/emission/index.htm.

National Intelligence Council. 2004. Mapping the global future: report on of the National Intelligence Council's 2020 project. Available at: http://www.dni.gov/nic/NIC_globaltrend2020.html.

Prentice, I.C.; Farquhar, G.D.; Fasham, M.J.R.; and others. 2001. The carbon cycle and atmospheric carbon dioxide. Chapter 3 in: Houghton, J.T.; Ding, Y.; Griggs, D.J.; Noguer, M.; van der Linden, P.J.; Dai, X.; Maskell, K.; Johnson, C.A., eds. Climate change 2001: the scientific basis. Contribution of Working Group I to the Third Assessment Report of the Intergovernmental Panel on Climate Change. Cambridge, United Kingdom and New York: Cambridge University Press. 881 p.

Price, D.T.; McKenney, D.W.; Papadopol, P.; Logan, T.; Hutchinson, M.F. 2004. High resolution future scenario climate data for North America. Pages 7.7-7.7.13 In: Proceedings of the 26th Conference on Agricultural and Forest Meteorology: Vancouver, British Columbia:, 23–26 August 2004. Boston, Massachusetts: American Meteorology Society. Available at: http://ams.confex.com/ams/AFAPURBBIO/techprogram/paper_78202.htm. [Accessed 28 July 2010.]

Price, D.T.; McKenney, D.W.; Joyce, L.A.; Siltanen, R.M.; Papadopol, P.; Lawrence, K. 2011. High-resolution interpolation of climate scenarios for Canada derived from General Circulation Model simulations. Inf. Rep. NOR-X-421. Edmonton, Alberta: Natural Resources Canada, Canadian Forest Service, Northern Forestry Center. 126 p.

Randall, D.A.; Wood, R.A.; Bony, S.; and others. 2007. Climate models and their evaluation. In: Solomon, S.; Qin, D.; Manning, M.; Chen, Z.; Marquis, M.; Averyt, K.B.; Tignor M.; Miller, H.L., eds. Climate change 2007: the physical science basis. Contribution of Working Group I to the Fourth Assessment Report of the Intergovernmental Panel on Climate Change. Cambridge, United Kingdom and New York: Cambridge University Press.

Ray, A.J.; Barsugli, J.J.; Wolter, K.; Eischeid, J.K. 2010. Rapid-response climate assessment to support the FWS status review of the American pika. Boulder, Colorado: NOAA Earth Systems Research Laboratory. Available at: http://www.esrl.noaa.gov/psd/news/2010/pdf/pika_report_final.pdf.

Reichler, Thomas; Junsu, Kim. 2008. How well do coupled models simulate today's climate? Bulletin of the American Meteorological Society 89:303-311.

United Nations Environment Program [UNEP]. 2002. Global Environment Outlook 3. London: Earthscan Publications Ltd. 460 p.

United Nations Environment Program [UNEP]. 2007. Global Environment Outlook 4. Valletta, Malta: Progress Press Ltd. 572 p.

U.S. Census Bureau. 2004. U.S. interim projections by age, sex, race and Hispanic origin. Internet release: March 18, 2004. Available online at: http://www.census.gov/population/www/projections/usinterimproj/natprojtab01a.pdf

U.S. Department of Commerce. 2008a. National income product accounts table 1.15. Gross domestic product. Version: January 30, 2008. Washington, DC: U.S. Department of Commerce, Bureau of Economic Analysis.

U.S. Department of Commerce. 2008b. National income product accounts table 2.1. Personal income and its disposition. Version: January 30, 2008. Washington, DC: U.S. Department of Commerce, Bureau of Economic Analysis.

U.S. Forest Service. 1977. The nation's renewable resources-an assessment, 1975. Forest Resource Report No. 21. Washington DC: U.S. Department of Agriculture, Forest Service, Washington Office. 243 p.

U.S. Forest Service. 1981. An assessment of the forest and range land situation in the United States. Forest Resource Report No. 22. Washington, DC: U.S. Department of Agriculture, Forest Service, Washington Office. 352 p.

U.S. Forest Service. 1989. RPA assessment of the forest and rangeland situation in the United States, 1989. Resource Report No. 26. Washington, DC: U.S. Department of Agriculture, Forest Service, Washington Office. 72 p.

U.S. Forest Service. 2001. 2000 RPA assessment of forest and range lands. FS-687. Washington DC: U.S. Department of Agriculture, Forest Service, Washington Office. 78 p.

Wear, David N. 2011. Forecasts of county-level land uses under three future scenarios: a technical document supporting the Forest Service 2010 RPA Assessment. Gen. Tech Rep-141. Asheville, North Carolina: U.S. Department of Agriculture, Forest Service, Southern Research Station. 41 p.

Wilby, R.L.; Charles, S.P.; Zorita, E.; Timbal, B.; Whetton, P.; Mearns, L.O. 2004. Guidelines for use of climate scenarios developed from statistical downscaling methods. Available at: http://www.ipcc-data.org/guidelines/dgm_no2_v1_09_2004.pdf.

Woods & Poole Economics Inc. 2006. The 2006 complete economic and demographic data source (CEDDS). Washington, DC. Available at: http://www.woodsandpoole.com.

Zarnoch, Stanley J.; Cordell, H. Ken; Betz, Carter J; Langner, Linda. 2010. Projecting county-level populations under three future scenarios: a technical document supporting the Forest Service 2010 RPA Assessment. E-Gen. Tech. Rep. SRS-128. Asheville, North Carolina: U.S. Department of Agriculture, Forest Service, Southern Research Station. 8 p.

26

USDA Forest Service Gen. Tech. Rep. RMRS-GTR-272. 2012

Appendix A—National Integrated Assessment Models

Six integrated assessment models (IAMs) were used to evaluate the emissions scenarios developed for the Intergovernmental Panel on Climate Change Third and Fourth Assessment Reports. This appendix briefly describes the six IAMs, based on Nakicenovic and others. (2000). More detailed descriptions of the models can be found at http://sedac.ciesin.org/mva/ and at references included in the individual model descriptions.

Asian Pacific Integrated Model

The Asian Pacific Integrated model (AIM) from the National Institute of Environmental Studies in Japan is a computer simulation model that was developed primarily to examine global warming responses in the Asia Pacific region but is linked to a world model that allows for global estimates. AIM includes three main models: a GHG emission model, a global change model, and a climate change impact model. The AIM model was used for the marker scenario for scenario A1B. Further documentation can be found in Morita and others (1994).

Atmospheric Stabilization Framework Model

The Atmospheric Stabilization Framework model (ASF) from ICF Consulting in the U.S.A. includes energy, agricultural, and deforestation GHG emissions and atmospheric models and provides emission estimates for nine world regions. The energy component is driven primarily by energy supply prices. The agricultural model estimates production of major agricultural products, driven by population and economic growth. The agricultural model is linked to a deforestation model that estimates deforestation related to population growth and demand for agricultural products. The outputs of these models are used to estimate GHG emissions. The atmospheric model uses the GHG emissions to calculate GHG concentrations and corresponding radiative forcing and temperature effects. The ASF model was used to develop the marker scenario for A2. Detailed documentation of the ASF model is found in Lashof and Tirpak (1990), Pepper and others (1992, 1998) and Sankovski and others (2000).

Integrated Model to Assess the Greenhouse Effect

The Integrated Model to Assess the Greenhouse Effect model (IMAGE2) from the National Institute for Public Health and Environmental Hygiene in the Netherlands has three linked sub-models. The Energy-Industry System computes GHG emissions in the 13 world regions of the model, based on a simulation model of energy investment decisions, using five economic sectors. The Terrestrial Environment System simulates global land-use and land-cover and their effect on GHG emissions and carbon fluxes between the biosphere and atmosphere. The Atmosphere-Ocean System uses a two-dimensional atmospheric energy model and a separate two-dimensional ocean model. Detailed documentation is available in Alcamo and others (1998) and de Vries and others (1994, 1999, 2000).

USDA Forest Service Gen. Tech. Rep. RMRS-GTR-272. 2012

27

Multiregional Approach for Resource and Industry Allocation

The Multiregional Approach for Resource and Industry Allocation model (MARIA) from the Science University of Tokyo in Japan is an integrated model designed to assess technology and policy options for addressing global climate change. MARIA is an intertemporal non-linear optimization model that allows international trading among eight global regions. An energy module includes three fossil fuels, biomass, nuclear power, and renewable energy sources. A food and land use module is used to assess the potential contributions of biomass. A global warming subsystem addresses global carbon emissions. Detailed documentation is available in Mori and Takahashi (1999) and Mori (2000).

Model for Energy Supply Strategy Alternatives and Their General Environmental Impact

The Model for Energy Supply Strategy Alternatives and Their General Environmental Impact model (MESSAGE) from the International Institute of Applied Systems Analysis (IIASA) in Austria is one of the six models that constitute IIASA's integrated modeling framework. Economic and energy development profiles are developed that serve as inputs for MESSAGE and their macro-economic model MACRO. MESSAGE is a dynamic linear programming model that calculates least-cost supply structures under the constraints of resource availability, available technologies, and demand for energy. MACRO estimates the relationships between macro-economic development and energy use. MESSAGE and MACRO are used in tandem to test scenario consistency. The marker scenario for B2 is based on MESSAGE. Further documentation can be found in Messner and Strubegger (1995) and Riahi and Roehrl (2000).

Mini Climate Assessment Model (MiniCAM)

The Mini Climate Assessment Model (MiniCAM) from the Pacific Northwest National Laboratory in the U.S.A. integrates three models. The Edmonds-Reilly-Barns energy-economic model represents long-term trends in economic output, energy use, and greenhouse gas emissions for nine world regions. The GHG emissions are used in the Model for the Assessment of Greenhouse-gas Induced Climate Change and the regional climate change Scenario Generator to provide estimates of atmospheric concentration, climate change, and sea level rise. More detailed documentation is found in Edmonds and others (1994, 1996a, 1996b).

Literature Cited

Alcamo, J.; Kreileman, E.; Krol, M.; Leemans, R.; Bollen, J.; van Minnen, J.; Schaefer, M.; Toet, S.; de Vries, B. 1998: Global modeling of environmental change: an overview of IMAGE 2.1. In Alcamo, J.; Leemans, R.; Kreileman, E., eds. Global change scenarios of the 21st century: results from the IMAGE 2.1 model. Kidlington, Oxford: Elsevier Science: pp. 3-94.

De Vries, B.; Bollen, J.; Bouwman, L.; den Elzen, M.; Janssen, M.; Kreileman, E. 2000. Greenhouse gas emissions in an equity-, environment- and service-oriented world: an IMAGE-based scenario for the next century. Technological Forecasting and Social Change 63(2-3).

De Vries, B.; Janssen, M.; Beusen, A. 1999. Perspectives on global energy futures-simulations with the TIME model. Energy Policy 27: 477-494.

De Vries, H.J.M.; Olivier, J.G.J.; van den Wijngaart, R.A.; Kreileman, G.J.J.; Toet, A.M.C. 1994. Model for calculating regional energy use, industrial production and greenhouse gas emissions for evaluating global climate scenarios. Water, Air and Soil Pollution 76: 79-131.

Edmonds, J.; Wise, M.; MacCracken, C. 1994. Advanced energy technologies and climate change: an analysis using the Global Change Assessment Model (GCAM). PNL-9798, UC-402, Richland, Washington: Pacific Northwest Laboratory.

Edmonds, J.; Wise, M.; Pitcher, H.; Richels, R.; Wigley, T.; MacCracken, C. 1996a. An integrated assessment of climate change and the accelerated introduction of advanced energy technologies: an application of MiniCAM 1.0. Mitigation and Adaptation Strategies for Global Change 1(4): 311-339.

Edmonds, J.; Wise, M.; Sands, R.; Brown, R.; Kheshgi, H. 1996b. Agriculture, land-use, and commercial biomass energy: a preliminary integrated analysis of the potential role of biomass energy for reducing future greenhouse related emissions. PNNL-11155. Washington, DC: Pacific Northwest National Laboratories.

Lashof, D.; Tirpak, D.A. 1990. Policy options for stabilizing global climate. 21P-2003. Washington, DC: U.S. Environmental Protection Agency.

Messner, S.; Strubegger, M. 1995. User's guide for MESSAGE III. WP-95- 69. Laxenburg, Austria: International Institute for Applied Systems Analysis.

Mori, S. 2000: The development of greenhouse gas emissions scenarios using an extension of the MARIA model for the assessment of resource and energy technologies. Technological Forecasting and Social Change 63(2-3).

Mori, S.; Takahashi, M. 1999. An integrated assessment model for the evaluation of new energy technologies and food productivity. International Journal of Global Energy Issues 11(1-4): 1-18.

Morita, Y.; Matsuoka, Y.; Kainuma, M.; Harasawa, H. 1994. AIM-Asian Pacific Integrated Model for evaluating policy options to reduce GHG emissions and global warming impacts. In: Bhattacharya, S.; and others, eds. Global warming issues in Asia. Bangkok: AIT: 254-273.

Pepper, W.J.; Barbour, W.; Sankovski, A.; Braaz, B. 1998. No-policy greenhouse gas emission scenarios: revisiting IPCC 1992. Environmental Science and Policy 1: 289-312.

Pepper, W.J.; Leggett, J.; Swart, R.; Wasson, J.; Edmonds, J.; Mintzer, I. 1992. Emissions scenarios for the IPCC: an update. In: Houghton, J.T.; Callandar, B.A.; Varney, S.K., eds. Climate change 1992: supplementary report to the IPCC scientific assessment. Cambridge: Cambridge University Press.

Riahi, K.; Roehrl, R.A. 2000: Greenhouse gas emissions in a dynamics-as-usual scenario of economic and energy development. Technological Forecasting and Social Change 63(2-3).

Sankovski, A.; Barbour, W.; Pepper, W. 2000. Quantification of the IS99 emission scenario storylines using the atmospheric stabilization framework (ASF). Technological Forecasting and Social Change 63(2-3).

USDA Forest Service Gen. Tech. Rep. RMRS-GTR-272. 2012

29

Appendix B—Definition of IPCC Macro Regions

OECD90 REGION		ASIA REGION	
North America (NAM)		**Centrally planned Asia and China (CPA)**	
Canada Guam Puerto Rico	United States of America Virgin Islands	Cambodia China Hong Kong Korea (DPR)	Laos (PDR) Mongolia Viet Nam
Western Europe (WEU)		**South Asia (SAS)**	
Andorra Austria Azores Belgium Canary Islands Channel Islands Cyprus Denmark Faeroe Islands Finland France Germany Gibraltar Greece Greenland Iceland	Ireland Isle of Man Italy Liechtenstein Luxembourg Madeira Malta Monaco Netherlands Norway Portugal Spain Sweden Switzerland Turkey	Afghanistan Bangladesh Bhutan India **Other Pacific Asia (PAS)** American Samoa Brunei Darussalam Fiji French Polynesia Gilbert-Kiribati Indonesia Malaysia Myanmar New Caledonia Papua New Guinea	Maldives Nepal Pakistan Sri Lanka Philippines Republic of Korea Singapore Solomon Islands Taiwan, province of China Thailand Tonga Vanuatu Western Samoa
Pacific OECD (PAO)			
Australia Japan	New Zealand		
REF REGION			
Central and Eastern Europe (EEU)		**Newly independent states of the former Soviet Union**	
Albania Bosnia and Herzegovina Bulgaria Croatia Czech Republic The former Yugoslav Republic of Macedonia	Hungary Poland Romania Slovak Republic Slovenia Yugoslavia	Armenia Azerbaijan Belarus Estonia Georgia Kazakhstan Kyrgyzstan Latvia	Lithuania Republic of Moldova Russian Federation Tajikistan Turkmenistan Ukraine Uzbekistan

Appendix B - continued			
ALM REGION			
Middle East and North Africa		*Latin America and the Caribbean*	
Algeria	Morocco	Antigua and Barbuda	Guyana
Bahrain	Oman	Argentina	Haiti
Egypt (Arab	Qatar	Bahamas	Honduras
Republic)	Saudi Arabia	Barbados	Jamaica
Iraq	Sudan	Belize	Martinique
Iran (Islamic	Syria (Arab	Bermuda	Mexico
Republic)	Republic)	Bolivia	Netherlands
Israel	Tunisia	Brazil	Antilles
Jordan	United Arab	Chile	Nicaragua
Kuwait	Emirates	Colombia	Panama
Lebanon	Yemen	Costa Rica	Paraguay
Libya/SPLAJ		Cuba	Peru
		Dominica	Saint Kitts and Nevis
Sub-Saharan Africa		Dominican Republic	Santa Lucia
		Ecuador	Saint Vincent and the
Angola	Malawi	El Salvador	Grenadines
Benin	Mali	French Guyana	Suriname
Botswana	Mauritania	Grenada	Trinidad and Tobago
British Indian	Mauritius	Guadeloupe	Uruguay
Ocean Territory	Mozambique	Guatemala	Venezuela
Burkina Faso	Namibia		
Burundi	Niger		
Cameroon	Nigeria		
Cape Verde	Reunion		
Central African	Rwanda		
Republic	Sao Tome		
Chad	and Principe		
Comoros	Senegal		
Cote d'Ivoire	Seychelles		
Congo	Sierra Leone		
Djibouti	Somalia		
Equatorial	South Africa		
Guinea	Saint Helena		
Eritrea	Swaziland		
Ethiopia	Tanzania		
Gabon	Togo		
Gambia	Uganda		
Ghana	Zaire		
Guinea	Zambia		
Guinea-Bissau	Zimbabwe		
Kenya			
Lesotho			
Liberia			
Madagascar			

USDA Forest Service Gen. Tech. Rep. RMRS-GTR-272. 2012

31

Appendix C—Availability of 2010 RPA Assessment Scenario Data

The detailed data on population, income, land use change, and climate described in this document are available to other users. This appendix provides links to those data sets.

Population, income, and land use data

County level projections of population, personal income, disposable personal income, and land use are available on the RPA Assessment website: http://www.fs.fed.us/research/rpa/pubs-supporting-2010-rpa-assessment.shtml. Population and income projections are provided in an Excel spreadsheet, including the 2006 base year data and projections from 2010 to 2060 at five-year intervals for all 50 States. The land use projections are provided on a separate Excel spreadsheet, with county level projections of cropland, pastureland, forest, range, and urban and developed land uses from 2010 to 2060 at 10-year intervals in the conterminous United States.

Climate data

The suite of projected climate variables (monthly mean daily maximum air temperature [°C], monthly mean daily minimum air temperature [°C], monthly total precipitation [mm], and computed values for potential evapotranspiration), downscaled to the 5 arc-minute grid and county scale, are available through the Forest Service archive website. The historical data spans 1990-2008 and the projection data spans the 2001 to 2100 period. Monthly data for each year is available. Meta-data documentation following international standards is available for each climate data set (Coulson and Joyce 2010a, 2010b; Coulson and others 2010a, 2010b, 2010 c, 2010d). The climate data, both historical and projected, are available at the RMRS archive web site: http://www.fs.fed.us/rm/data_archive/dataaccess/contents_location.shtml#US.

Literature Cited

Coulson, David P.; Joyce, Linda A. 2010a. Historical climate data (1940-2006) for the conterminous United States at the 5 arc minute grid spatial scale based on PRISM climatology. Fort Collins, Colorado: U.S. Department of Agriculture, Forest Service, Rocky Mountain Research Station. Available at: doi:10.2737/RDS-2010-0011.

Coulson, David P.; Joyce, Linda A. 2010b. Historical Climate data (1940-2006) for the conterminous United States at the county spatial scale based on PRISM climatology. Fort Collins, Colorado: U.S. Department of Agriculture, Forest Service, Rocky Mountain Research Station. Available at: doi:10.2737/RDS-2010-0010.

Coulson, David P.; Joyce, Linda A.; Price, David T.; McKenney, Daniel W. 2010a. Climate scenarios for the conterminous United States at the 5 arc minute grid spatial scale using SRES scenarios B2 and PRISM climatology. Fort Collins, Colorado: U.S. Department of Agriculture, Forest Service, Rocky Mountain Research Station. Available at: http://www.fs.fed.us/rm/data_archive/dataaccess/US_ClimateScenarios_grid_B2_PRISM.shtml.

Coulson, David P.; Joyce, Linda A.; Price, David T.; McKenney, Daniel W. 2010b. Climate scenarios for the conterminous United States at the county spatial scale using SRES scenarios B2 and PRISM climatology. Fort Collins, Colorado: U.S. Department of Agriculture, Forest Service, Rocky Mountain Research Station. Available at: doi:10.2737/RDS-2010-0009.

Coulson, David P.; Joyce, Linda A.; Price, David T.; McKenney, Daniel W.; Siltanen, R. Martin; Papadopol, Pia; Lawrence, Kevin. 2010c. Climate scenarios for the conterminous United States at the 5 arc minute grid spatial scale using SRES scenarios A1B and A2 and PRISM climatology. Fort Collins, Colorado: U.S. Department of Agriculture, Forest Service, Rocky Mountain Research Station. Available at: http://www.fs.fed.us/rm/data_archive/dataaccess/US_ClimateScenarios_grid_A1B_A2_PRISM.shtml.

32

USDA Forest Service Gen. Tech. Rep. RMRS-GTR-272. 2012

Coulson, David P.; Joyce, Linda A.; Price, David T.; McKenney, Daniel W.; Siltanen, R. Martin; Papadopol, Pia; Lawrence, Kevin. 2010d. Climate scenarios for the conterminous United States at the county spatial scale using SRES scenarios A1B and A2 and PRISM climatology. Fort Collins, Colorado: U.S. Department of Agriculture, Forest Service, Rocky Mountain Research Station. Available at: doi:10.2737/RDS-2010-0008.

Appendix D—Acronyms

AR4	IPCC 4th Assessment
DDC	IPCC Data Distribution Centre
DPI	Disposable personal income
ERS	Economic Research Service
FIA	Forest Inventory and Analysis
GCM	Global circulation model
GDP	Gross domestic product
GHG	Greenhouse gas
IAM	Integrated assessment model
IPCC	Intergovernmental Panel on·Climate Change
NRI	National Resources Inventory
OECD90	IPCC macro region that includes the United States (See Appendix B)
PCPI	Per capita personal income
RPA	Forest and Rangeland Renewable Resources Planning Act
TAR	Third IPCC Assessment
UNEP	United Nations Environmental Program
USD	United States dollar
WP	Wood-Poole Economics, Inc.